A
Practical
Career Guide
for
Criminal
Justice
Professionals

Take
Charge of
Your
Career!

Michael Carpenter
Roger Fulton

L L P **L**ooseleaf
Law Publications, Inc.

43-08 162nd Street • Flushing, NY 11358
www.LooseleafLaw.com • 800-647-5547

2nd Printing - 2008

ISBN: 978-1-932777-42-0

Library of Congress Cataloging-in-Publication Data

Carpenter, Michael J.
  A practical career guide for criminal justice professionals : take charge of your career / Michael Carpenter and Roger Fulton.
    p. cm.
  ISBN-13: 978-1-932777-42-0
  1. Criminal justice, Administration of--Vocational guidance--United States.
I. Fulton, Roger. II. Title.
  HV9950.C37 2007
  364.973023--dc22   2007026562

Contents

About the Authors

Michael Carpenter

Michael Carpenter has more than thirty years experience in various criminal justice related positions, having worked with a municipal police department, a state police agency, as a state-wide police specialist for the State of New York, and is currently a full-time professor of criminal justice at Adirondack Community College in upstate New York.

He started his career with a city police department, and then worked with a state police agency for more than ten years as a trooper, as an investigator, and as a sergeant. Later hired by the State of New York as a "police training specialist," he assisted in developing and implementing the country's first state-sponsored law enforcement accreditation program. He assisted more than 65 agencies achieve accreditation or re-accreditation status. For several years, he also prepared detailed management studies of police departments for the State of New York and offered specific recommendations to resolve various administrative or operational issues that these agencies faced.

In addition to practical experience, he holds a Masters' Degree in Criminal Justice and a Masters' Degree in Teaching, and has more than ten years experience in supervisory and administrative positions. He has been a certified police instructor for more than twenty years, and was an adjunct college instructor for more than ten years.

He has written several books, edited several books, has had more than 100 articles or columns published in national criminal justice publications, has taught in college classrooms, made presentations at national conferences and worked as a private consultant. He is also the founder of a successful police consulting service called *Police Management Services*. He can be contacted through his webpage at *www.policemanagement.com*.

Roger Fulton
Captain, New York State Police (Ret.)

Roger Fulton has dedicated himself to police professionalism for more than thirty years. He quickly rose through the ranks of the New York State Police to the rank of captain. During his career, he held numerous command and administrative positions.

Roger holds a Ph.D. in Criminal Justice Management, a Masters' Degree in Criminal Justice and is a graduate of the FBI's National Academy (139th Session). In addition to his education and training, he has years of practical supervisory and management experience in both the public and private sectors. In recent years, he has traveled extensively from Florida to Alaska and from California to New Jersey as a consultant, advisor and trainer for police departments and academies throughout the nation.

He is the author of three successful books, *Common Sense Supervision, Common Sense Leadership*, and *Practical Law Enforcement Management*. He was also a columnist for *Law Enforcement Technology Magazine* for twelve years writing on police supervision, management and leadership issues.

He can be contacted through his webpage at: *www.Roger Fulton.com*.

CHAPTER 1

Introduction

This is a career development guide for those who want to excel in a criminal justice agency. It consists of a series of short and practical chapters that will help you take control of your career, earn repeated promotions and prepare yourself to have a successful career in your criminal justice agency and beyond. Consider this career guide as a blueprint of how to build your own successful career.

In some corporate environments, you meet a career counselor soon after you are hired and they ask you about your career aspirations with the company. They ask you where you want to be in five years, ten years and twenty years. Based on your answers, they recommend a career path of education and experience that will help you reach your goals. Periodically they check in with you to see how you are proceeding along your selected career path.

Well, in most criminal justice agencies in the United States there are no such career counselors. It is almost entirely up to you to identify a career path, and then figure out how to get there—often with little or no support from your agency. You decide on your own what combination of education, training and experience you need to succeed in your agency, and you figure out how to get what you need to be successful. It can be very frustrating.

In this career guide, we will try to help you make good career choices for yourself. We will provide you with advice and direction so that you will feel that you have some control over your career five years, ten years and twenty years ahead. We will help you develop skills in your current position that will help you prepare for your next promotion. We can help you develop the skills and confidence to perform your job at every rank with calm confidence because you know that you are prepared and can make good decisions. And finally, you will enjoy a long and successful career with progressively higher pay, better benefits and ultimately, a comfortable pension check every month after you retire.

CHAPTER 2

You and Your Current Position

Since today is the first day of your new career, it's time to stop and think about where you are in your career. Whether you are looking for a job in criminal justice, currently employed but looking for another job in criminal justice, or looking to get on the fast-track in your current position, it's still time to take a look at where you are and plan where you are going. After all, you can't decide where you need to go or how to get there unless you know where you are starting from.

So, it is time to take an inventory of yourself, your qualifications and preferences, and where you want to go in the future. There are many diverse and interesting jobs in the criminal justice system and you have to choose the career path that is right for you, now and in the future. So get out a piece of paper and make some notes as we lead you down a path toward your personal inventory.

Who are you?

First, it's time to assess some of your core qualities and personality traits to decide where you might fit into the criminal justice system. As an example, if you like to smoke marijuana, drink to excess and routinely disregard the law, then you will enter the criminal justice system automatically over time—but from the wrong end! (Don't laugh . . . we talked with a detective a while ago who was doing a background investigation on a police officer applicant. Through a polygraph and background investigation, it was determined that the prospective recruit had smoked marijuana *at least* two hundred times in the previous five years!)

Criminal justice personnel are generally honest and law-abiding, with a solid and practical sense of right and wrong. They generally are willing to conform to agency standards, dress appropriately and follow the rules. They have a strong work ethic and a genuine desire to help people and to make the world a better place. If your ethics and personality fit into these categories, then you should be in the criminal justice system in some capacity. If you don't fit into these categories, then even if you get hired in your "dream job," you will soon be viewed as a liability to that agency and they will do their best to get rid of you.

What is your risk level?

Many jobs in criminal justice involve both physical and career risks. Street level police officers, corrections officers and other "front line" employees, who go into "harm's way" every day, face the potential for physical confrontations and unknown risks daily. Their careers can end in an instant through death, injury or a bad decision. It's not exciting . . . it's not glamorous . . . it's not like a hyped-up "cops in a high speed chase" show on TV. It is dangerous, risky, and a split-second wrong decision by you can end your career very fast. Are you willing to take those kinds of risks? Is your family willing to take those kinds of risks?

On the other hand, there are many other jobs in criminal justice jobs that involve less risk, but still more risk than most citizens face at their daily jobs. For example, some probation/parole officers carry weapons and are trained in defensive tactics. And, of course, there are many administrative or civilian positions in criminal justice that have little or no risk. Only you can assess the perceived risks of a job, and your willingness to subject you and your family to those risks. Decide where you stand on this issue before going any further. Answer honestly and thoughtfully.

What is your education level?

Is writing reports pure drudgery for you? If so, is it a problem with your attitude or a lack of grammar and spelling skills? If it is any of these problems, then you may want to stay away from some career paths. Investigative positions generally require substantial amounts of paperwork and reports. Supervisory positions always require reports, performance evaluations and excellent written and oral communication skills.

The higher up you go in almost any criminal justice agency, the more paperwork there is, the more attention to detail is required, the more accountability there is and often the more liability there is. Almost every job in criminal justice involves enormous amounts of paperwork, and it must be done correctly, professionally and on time.

Realistically assess your personal skills levels right now to decide whether or not to pursue these kinds of career paths. If you don't have the skills now, you may need to get more education to improve them before moving ahead. If you honestly don't have the necessary skills, and are unwilling to go back to school to improve them, then make the decision to stay where you are most comfortable.

Do you want to lead others?

In order to succeed in any supervisory position, you must have the *will to lead* others. Without that desire, you may be destined to be a poor or mediocre manager at best. At worst, you will be unhappy, your people will be miserable and you will have a long, lonely and unsatisfying career . . . if you last!

If you don't want to lead others, you can still have a very good career in criminal justice by just being the best you can be and being responsible just for your own performance. Evidence technicians, lab analysts, K-9 handlers and many other "technical" jobs are available and require no supervisory duties on your part. That may be the career path you want to take. The pay may be a little lower, and you may limit your long-term career growth, but you will be much happier in that career path.

There are many other questions you need to ask yourself about specific jobs, but we have covered some of the main ones here. Others might include your willingness to travel, to relocate, to be un-armed, or to be armed, to use force against someone, to work odd shifts and long hours. These are all decisions that you will have to make. But the first step in all of this is to know who YOU are and what you are willing to do, or not do.

So, take some time to think about who you are before you move on in this guide. Then, if you are still interested in moving up the ranks, read on!

Stop now and review this chapter. Think about, and make some notes about the following questions:

1. Who are you?
2. What is your risk level?
3. What is your educational level?
4. Do you want to lead others?

This is the time to evaluate and make solid decisions before you move on to the rest of this guide!

CHAPTER 3

Working Toward Promotions

Your preparation for promotion starts now! Too many people think that it starts when an opening occurs or a promotional exam is announced. Trust us—those who think that way are not likely to be promoted. They will already be far behind the professionals, like you, who have been thinking ahead and preparing themselves for a long time. For you, the time until the exam or oral boards will just be your final "kick" to the finish line.

Preparing for promotion should start during your basic training program. For many criminal justice professionals, that means in the Academy. At that stage of your career, you will be presented with all the basics of the laws, your role, your agency's role and what is expected of you and others in the organization. Work hard to learn everything you can while there, for you will repeatedly see those ideals in both your everyday work, as well as on future promotional exams. Also, you can set yourself apart from your fellow employees at this early stage by applying yourself completely to your work, by being viewed as a role model and by developing skills like leadership, assertiveness, public speaking, etc. It's nice to start your career in criminal justice as "class president" or "high academic award" for your training class.

Once out in the field, there are many steps that you can take to enhance your reputation, as well as continually preparing for future promotions. In the past, good common sense was thought to be the number one attribute necessary for success in a criminal justice agency at any rank. Good common sense is still important, but knowledge of ever-increasing complex laws, personnel policies and litigation prevention tactics are all just as necessary.

In the new millennium, progressive and upwardly mobile

criminal justice personnel will reach out and take charge of their careers. They recognize that the minimal training mandated in some states can result in minimal performance, and they want more. They want a successful career with progressively more money, responsibility and prestige. They want a career that serves them well for 20–30 years, and then provide them with a substantial income in their retirement years.

These progressive officers look to a well-balanced career development process to set themselves apart from their peers. They are preparing themselves for success and will be ready when opportunities arise. This balanced approach involves the three keys to success; education, training and experience, and is a basic guide for any upwardly mobile criminal justice professional, regardless of their current rank or title. Other tactics and affiliations can also help you build a successful career.

Education

We strongly believe that the more education that you have, the better the chances of your success in the field of criminal justice. Many criminal justice jobs currently require a strong college background just to apply. For example, the minimum qualifications for a probation officer in our part of the country are a Bachelor's Degree and three years of experience, or a Masters' Degree. Of course, other jobs will have varying amounts of education.

We have found that municipal law enforcement and corrections tend to have the least amount of education required to apply. But of course that does not mean a person should expect to get hired with the minimum. For example, we recently spoke with a newly-hired state trooper, and he told us something that only reinforces our belief in more education. He told us that the minimum educational requirement to take the state police test in his state is a high school diploma. But, of all the recruits attending the state police academy that he was in, all but one recruit had a Bachelor's Degree . . . and that recruit had a Master's Degree.

Formal education is becoming the norm in criminal justice jobs, whether by officially raising the minimum educational levels to apply for a position, or by unofficially not considering an applicant who only meets the minimums. And certainly, more and more criminal justice jobs are expecting candidates to have formal education to get promoted. That just makes sense. If the new employees are expected to have a high level of education to get hired (whether officially or unofficially), then supervisors and administrators are expected to have a *higher* level of education (whether officially or unofficially) than the employees they supervise. The more education you have, the better! And, of course, the more education you have, the better your chances of moving on to a successful job after you retire.

Your future is up to you on this issue. Spend some of your off-duty hours watching sitcoms on TV, or spend them in a classroom. It's pretty easy to figure out which will improve your chances of having a successful career!

Training

Here is something to remember: training budgets are limited in most criminal justice agencies, and there is often competition for the limited number of training opportunities that agencies have. Therefore, it makes sense that administrators will pick the best candidates for the limited training programs that they schedule. Here is a question for you to think about—why should your boss send you to one of these limited (and potentially career-boosting) training programs? What skills, talents and abilities have you shown day-in and day-out in your current position that would set you apart from the other people who all want to go to the same training program? It is not enough to *want* to go to a training program—you often have to *earn* the privilege to go. If the boss views you as an asset to your agency, as someone who has shown the "right stuff," and someone who he can rely on to get the most out of the training, then he *may* pick you.

If you are picked to go to a training program, take advantage of *every* training opportunity that comes along. It doesn't matter if it is in the middle of hunting season and you are an avid hunter, or if it's in the first week in January and you usually take a cruise to the Caribbean that week. Training classes are rare in some agencies, and for the boss to pick you to go to a certain training class is called "an opportunity." You know about opportunity knocking?

Obviously, every training class that you go to will add to your resume, make you a more informed criminal justice professional and improve your career. A bonus to this, however, is the ability to meet other hand-picked criminal justice professionals from other agencies at these training programs. Whether these training seminars are held twenty miles away from you or across the country, you will meet up-and-coming people, like yourself, whom you may remain in contact with for many years after. The importance of networking cannot be emphasized too many times!

Experience

The amount of experience an employee has is not solely a function of how long they have on the job. The types of experience they gain will vary from individual to individual. In many criminal justice agencies, the length and type of experience you gain is something you can control, at least to some degree. Working a busy area as a police officer, or as a supervisor, can help you quickly gain valuable experience. Often "lazy" employees look to work in the assignments that are "slow" or don't have a lot of responsibility. But, more successful employees often ask to work in the "busy" units or seek new assignments regularly to learn as much as they can as fast as they can. These assignments can also help you to learn from the failures and successes of the people you work with in such a busy area. Don't hesitate to get involved and ask questions. It's better for you to learn from someone else's mistake than your own.

As you move through your career, you should make every effort to diversify your experiences. This will prevent career burn-out, will give you more overall knowledge of your agency, and will improve your chances of promotion. If you get labeled as someone who only knows one or two aspects of the job, then you are of little value to the organization. Plan your career so that you move between assignments every few years, and this may even include giving up an assignment that you like and transferring to an assignment that you may not care too much about.

Professional associations

Upwardly mobile criminal justice professionals participate in trade associations to receive up-to-date information in the field as well as to "network" with other professionals in their particular field.

These organizations often provide magazines and newsletters that discuss current issues, problems, solutions and trends within the industry. Most also have an annual trade show where you can meet face-to-face with other members of your profession from across the state or across the country, as well as learn what is new in the particular technology, products and procedures of your chosen profession. Virtually every criminal justice specialty has these associations and trade shows. Some examples are specific trade publications and shows for dispatchers, police officers, correction officers, court officers, gang units, victim's rights advocates, prosecutors, defense attorneys and chiefs of police. There are many more. Use your investigative skills to seek and find the ones in your industry that will suit you best.

We suggest that you spend maybe $200 or $300 a year to join professional associations and subscribe to several professional journals. By reading these journals, by finding out what other agencies are doing across the country, by keeping current with legal updates, you will become much better informed than your co-workers. Your boss will soon see that you are serious about your career, and your fellow employees may soon start looking to you for answers and guidance. At that point, you become a much more valuable asset to your agency.

Writing

As you acquire certain knowledge about your job, it is natural that you would want to share this with your co-workers. This makes you a more valuable member of your agency, makes people appreciate you as a team-player and a trainer, and should make you feel good that you are helping other people.

Now, there are several ways that you can share your job knowledge. If you are lucky, your agency may assign you to be a training officer for new employees, or maybe one of your co-workers will ask you to help them. But this is pretty random and you are limited in how many people you share your job knowledge with. You should reach as many people as possible to try and help them do their job better. We know how you can!

Write what you have to share down on paper and get it published in a magazine or journal that your peers across the state or country will read. That way, you can help many of your peers all at the same time. No . . . don't laugh . . . .we're serious! There are dozens of criminal justice magazines and journals that are published every month, and they are always looking for articles. And, even if you have never written anything more than an investigative report for your agency, you can get something published.

With a little bit of work on your part, this knowledge that you are sharing with your fellow criminal justice professionals across the country can get you recognition, add to your resume, improve your chances of getting promoted and give you a big boost of confidence. Seems like you can't lose.

Speaking

Public speaking is a big part of any criminal justice job. From your very first oral interview to get hired, through the various interviews you face to get promoted, to the formal presentations that you may have to make to civic groups, politicians, the media, etc. as you go through the ranks, your career often depends on how well you speak in public.

Of course, if you are thinking about how this can improve your chances of a successful career in criminal justice, public speaking is a critical skill in getting promoted. Whether your agency uses an oral board, an assessment center or other variations as part of the promotional process, you need to do well in these tests or you will not get promoted. We recommend that no matter where you are in your career, that you improve your public speaking skills now so that you will be that much better prepared than your competition when you get the notice for your next promotional oral board.

If your agency does not give you the opportunity to practice this skill, then make your own opportunities. For example, you can take a public speaking course at a nearby college. You can offer to work with the public relations people in your criminal justice agency. If your agency does not have a public relations unit, let your boss know that you would like to volunteer to make presentations, if anyone from the community should ask. You could also consider joining a group called "Toastmaster's International," that specializes in developing public speaking skills for anyone who wants to sign up. We highly recommend joining!

If this is one of your weaknesses, you need to work on it before it is exposed at the wrong time and embarrasses you or hurts your career.

Training/Teaching

If you attended a basic training class when you were hired in criminal justice, do you remember the instructors who taught at that academy? Were they sharp, professional and did you admire them for the knowledge that they shared with you? Well, have you ever thought about applying to be a trainer? Most training academies are looking for criminal justice employees to teach a block of instruction. How good would that look on your resume? Or, what about being a trainer for some in-service training classes that your agency may sponsor? This is another great way to share your knowledge and expertise with your fellow criminal justice professionals. (As a personal note, one of the main reasons that I developed an interest in training when I first entered criminal justice was because I had such poor instructors at the basic police training academy that I went to. I thought: "Even *I* could do a better job than *he's* doing!" Less than two years later, I taught my first training class for my agency.)

Another opportunity for you to share your skills, knowledge and abilities is to consider teaching criminal justice classes at a nearby college. The standards to teach, even part-time, at most colleges include at least a Master's Degree, years of practical knowledge and the ability to teach. But, this is one example of how you can be rewarded by combining several of the skills that we previously mentioned—a college degree, public speaking, publishing . . . it all ties together nicely!

Okay, so you agree that getting your degrees, going to all kinds of training classes, getting diversified experience, getting published and even becoming a trainer is the way to a successful career. Now you ask, "Where do I get the time for all this and still do my job?"

Here is where common sense prevails. First, building a successful career IS your job. And, like any job, it takes persistence, determination, motivation and some sacrifice. But, the rewards can be worth it. Second, start now! You've got 20–30 years to get all the education, training, and experience you can handle. Map out a long-range career plan to guide you. If you are not comfortable planning out goals and objectives, find a successful person in your agency (or that you know personally), and find out what they did, how they did it and what they recommend for your career plan.

You don't need it all "right away," you can get it "on your way," but don't let personal fears, excuses or other distractions get "in your way."

REVIEW QUESTIONS:

1. If entry-level officers at your agency are required to have a two-year college degree, why is it important that supervisors have more than a two-year degree?

2. What is the danger of becoming too specialized in one particular area? How can you avoid being over-specialized?

3. Why should upwardly mobile officers join professional associations?

4. Why is public speaking a skill that you should master? What are three ways that you can develop these skills?

5. Where will you find time for all of this career-building and still do your job?

CHAPTER 4

Preparing for Promotional Exams and Oral Boards

In the criminal justice field, nearly every rung on the ladder of success involves taking a written exam and usually some other testing criteria such as an oral interview. We have heard too many candidates at entry level and promotional level say: "I don't do well on tests." Well, of course you don't if you don't prepare for those tests. Success goes to the well-prepared.

All of the entry level or promotional level exams, whether written or oral, will relate directly to the job you are applying for in the criminal justice system. At entry-level, you will be tested on your aptitude for criminal justice work. You will be tested for reading comprehension, observation skills, decision-making, and even skills related to following orders and discipline. At the promotional level, you will be tested for your knowledge of agency policies, as well as supervisory and leadership knowledge and ability.

Virtually all of the skills necessary to succeed can be learned or improved on, if you are willing to put in the time and effort! So in the following pages, we shall suggest tips to help you be successful in both written and oral examinations. The rest is up to you!

Policies, procedures and laws

At the promotional-level, both written and oral examinations are designed to test your ability to know, understand and apply the policies, procedures and applicable laws appropriate to your agency. So, if you want to succeed, know them!

Most progressive agencies have extensive policy and procedure manuals that are issued to each employee. Study them... understand them . . . be ready to apply them to both everyday and exceptional situations. As an example: when can a supervisor relieve an employee from duty for drug use . . . for how long . . . can you order the employee to take a drug test . . . what rights does the employee have . . . what tests can the supervisor administer at the time . . . what is the reporting/investigative process for the supervisor . . . etc . . . etc?

The laws that relate to your section of the criminal justice system are easily obtained. Many agencies provide their employees with the pertinent sections of the criminal law, criminal procedure law, and any other laws related to job responsibility and performance. The biggest problem we have seen is that many employees don't keep their policy manuals up-to-date. Oh, well . . . those employees usually remain in their current position and don't get promoted.

Here we offer a few tips about how to stay up-to-date with your policies, procedures and laws.

- Study hard in your basic training course. Learn all you can. That will be your foundation for your career. Employees who start out in their careers as mediocre recruits often end up as mediocre employees, and sometimes end up as mediocre bosses. Not good!

- Look up things as they occur to you and to your fellow employees. Be sure you know the "why's" and "how's" of what happens as new situations occur in your workplace.

- Ask questions about situations, and then learn to answer your own questions. "Why was that guy charged with 'Burglary Second Degree' instead of 'Burglary First Degree'? Be sure you know why. If you don't know for sure, look it up. Still not sure? Ask somebody who knows (. . . make sure they know what they are talking about first, before you take it as gospel). Once you get the right explanation, double-check it in the criminal law or in your agency's policy manual. (It isn't that you don't believe them, but this way you are using more senses—listening, talking and reading—to improve your learning.)

- Read all new memos, training bulletins, general orders or anything else that comes to your attention. Study them carefully. You may even want to make a copy of the material for your personal "study file." New material is one source of both written and oral exam questions. Set yourself apart from the other candidates by being up-to-date on the hot topics in your agency and in the field of criminal justice.

Anticipate the exam

Many criminal justice agencies give ninety days notice for promotional examinations. Typically, most candidates then start to worry . . . a few weeks later some of them start to gather study material . . . a few weeks later some of them actually open the study material to look at it . . . and then a week or so before the actual test date, they start cramming. Sound familiar?

Simple logic should tell you that the promotional exam will be based on many of the same topics from the previous exam, and that includes policies, procedures and laws. So look ahead to get ahead. Only fools wait for that ninety-day notice. While you are in your current position, think ahead, and work ahead. While others open their policy and procedure manuals for the first time and frantically search for all the new updates, you have already been studying your manual for months. By the time the announcement comes out, all you have to do is refresh your knowledge with the most recent changes in policies or laws—not a complete refresher from the previous two or three years. You have already studied the existing laws, policies and procedures, anticipated the material to be covered, and you already have a substantial study advantage over those "90-days and I'm starting to worry" co-workers, who have waited too long to adequately study for their chance for success.

Past exams/Other exams

The promotional exam that you will be facing is not likely to be the first time an exam like this has been given for that position. Therefore, there is some history about the exam and the examination process you can learn about, if you take the time to look for it.

Regarding written exams, there may be copies of past exams floating around somewhere in your agency. If there are, round up as many as possible and then make them a part of your study program. Although the questions may change, they can still give you some insight into how the exam writers are thinking, and what the priorities might be for that promotional position.

Toward the end of your study period, you can also use these old exams as practice for taking the real exams. Set up the "mock exams" just like the real ones, by allotting the proper time for the various sections, such as multiple-choice questions, math section, reading comprehension, etc.

If the previous exams were oral exams, you may be able to get some idea about the questions that were asked from previous candidates, both the successful AND the unsuccessful ones. Not only will you be able to prepare for similar or the same questions, you will also get a "feel" for what types of questions oral boards might ask. This system can also work for previous written exam questions as well, when no other source is available. For example, if you are not eligible to take a test, listen carefully to your co-workers who did, as they talk about the test and the specific questions on the test. You may want to take notes about the questions and file these notes away until you need them to prepare for your own test.

Don't rule out the use of other department's exams for a similar position. As an example, the laws, policies and procedures and the decision-making questions for the first-line supervisor's position are likely to be similar across similar criminal justice agencies. Contact any friends you may have from other departments to see what is available to them, as well as their experiences as successful or unsuccessful candidates for that position.

Over the years, there have been retired officers who have written books containing sample questions for candidates for supervisory positions. Seek them out. They will give you insights into what examiners may be looking for and you might even find one or more of the exact questions you will face on your own exam. Also, take the time to seek out professional advice, often in book form, on how to prepare for and take exams, including how to do well facing an oral board. These books can include information on how to prepare and take an "in basket exercise" or assessment center, if that is a part of your agency's testing and evaluation program. (As an example,

Looseleaf Law Publications—publishers of this book—have more than 45 resources for you in the area of "Promotion and Testing Aids.")

The exam announcement

Hopefully, you will be well prepared when the exam announcement is released. There are usually ninety days before the actual exam date, but that varies from agency to agency, When the notice is posted, get a copy of it and make it part of your study material. Read and re-read it carefully and make a list of what you need to do to comply with it.

Generally, the announcement will give a job description of the position and the minimum qualifications an individual must have to be eligible to take the test. Check these eligibility requirements very carefully to be sure that you meet them. They may have changed from past announcements. Check the length of time that you must be employed by your agency to take the test, the amount of time required in your current position, or any college degrees or other requirements. Prove to yourself, in writing, that you meet all of the eligibility requirements and be ready to provide documentation to anyone who asks for this proof. That includes entry dates, promotion dates, diplomas, transcripts and documented experience in previous positions. Don't get denied a testing opportunity because of a missing piece of paper, or because you lack a requirement, or because you can't find your old high school or college diploma. (And it doesn't matter whether it is your fault or your agency's fault that the piece of paper is missing, you still may miss the test and may have to wait years before it comes around again!)

The announcement may also list the books and manuals that some of the exam questions may be taken from. This list is almost sure to include your agency's policy and procedure manual. There may also be sources listed for local, state and federal laws and court decisions. For most management positions, there may be management textbooks listed, as well. There may be a catch-all phrase, such as: "Candidates must have a demonstrated knowledge of all appropriate laws, policies, procedures and management techniques for the position." Translate that as you will, but . . . you had better know everything in every book that is on that book list.

Re-read the announcement and make a list of all the manuals and texts that are mentioned. Then, go get them! Don't worry about the price. Promotions are generally worth thousands of dollars a year in pay, thousands of dollars for each year after you are promoted, and thousands of dollars a year in future retirement pay. Spend what you must to get up-to-date books. Check your list to be sure that you get the correct editions. Textbooks often release new editions every few years. Pay what you have to for the most current edition. And, act immediately to get your books. Too many candidates have been "shut out" by books that are sold out and may not be available for 6–8 weeks. Act now!

If you are not eligible for a promotional test this time around, you should still read the announcement. You should be planning for your time, even if it is several years away. For example, you can get copies of the textbooks that are listed and start reading through them at your leisure. Becoming more familiar with your policy manual and laws and court decisions certainly won't hurt you. This "extra" knowledge that you acquire will not be wasted, as hopefully it will make you better at the position you are now in, and it will give you a strong background to build on when the next test that you are eligible for comes around.

Here are some other tips. If there is any question about whether your copies of any law book or policy manual are up-to-date or possibly incomplete, act now to get the most current material. The announcement should state: "Laws and procedures as in effect on a 'given date'. Don't be ahead or behind on these kinds of dates or your answers will be marked wrong!

Study, study, study

If you have been listening to our advice about preparing yourself before the exam announcement, you now have about ninety days to hone your skills and knowledge to prove what you know. Consider this last ninety days as the "sprint kick" of a long race that you have been running for many months or years now.

Right now, your primary focus is to get yourself promoted. Yes, you will still be working at your current job, but make a substantial effort to focus on that exam and getting promoted. Consider this a part-time job! Study on-duty and off-duty as you can. Your friends on-duty may take some of your other tasks when they know you are going for promotion. Your supervisor may assign you less demanding assignments, and, your family needs to understand that you may not be available as much for the next ninety days for them.

Don't just study randomly. Make a realistic plan you can live with. Break the policy manual up into one-hour study segments. Break the laws up into similar study segments. Schedule the study of the management or supervision texts by chapter. Put your plan into a written schedule that you can start on and stick with for the next few months. Hit your weakest areas first and longest.

Study everything, including the footnotes. Outline the chapters if writing things down helps you remember things (. . . it does for most people, whether we like to admit it or not). Make up acronyms to help you remember the elements of a crime or the steps to follow for a certain procedure. Visualize the statutes that case laws come out of to help you remember them. Make study notes on critical numbers, dates, definitions, etc. Some candidates turn these notes into flash cards they can study when they have a few minutes on a break or over lunch.

Prepare for exam day well before exam day. Follow the rules listed in the announcement. Can you bring a calculator to the test? Do you need pencils or pens? If pen, what color ink? What about erasers? Do you need identification or any other documentation? Settle these issues well in advance of exam day. Check with your personnel office, and then bring a couple of everything that you could possibly need to the test.

The night before the exam, get a good night's sleep if you can. Set two alarm clocks, one with a battery back-up. Arrange a back-up transportation plan, in case you have a dead battery or flat tire. Allow extra time for auto accidents, flat tires and anything else that could possibly go wrong (. . . do you know about Murphy's Law?). If that exam starts without you, you may have to wait several years to take the next one.

Once you get to the test site, stay calm and look over the entire exam briefly to be sure that there are no missing pages or other surprises. Make a plan to finish each segment in a given amount of time so you can finish well within the allotted time. Allow some time to go back to questions you skipped over or want to go back and check. Spend any extra time reviewing your test. Check to be sure there are no blank spaces. Check to be sure that your answers are in the right places and are clearly marked. This is especially important if you skip some questions during the test and then continue on filling in answers. When the test is over, you are done. Go home to your family and make up for lost time. The results won't be out for an eternity (often six to eight weeks), and it's too late to go back and change anything.

Oral boards

If you score well on the written exam, you may have to face an oral board interview. Or, if a written exam isn't required, you may face just the oral interview. There are many types of oral exams, including videotaped exam scenarios, in-basket exercises, assessment centers, and/or facing an oral interview with several senior members from within or outside of your agency.

Your best chances for success are by doing everything we have previously talked about. Do your homework, prepare and study. Follow the rules listed in the original test announcement, as well as keeping any documents that you received inviting you to the oral board. Obviously, dress appropriately. You will never get a second chance to make a first impression on this oral board.

During your interview, make eye contact and shake hands with each member of the oral board as you are introduced and vice versa. If you shake hands, do it the right way (neither too soft nor too firm) Listen to all instructions carefully. For example: they may suggest that you go over to a nearby table and get a glass of water ". . . and use one of the overturned glasses . . ." Pay attention . . . that's a trick question for you to see if you are listening!

When you are asked a question, take a short moment to formulate your answer. Remain calm and answer the question to the best of your ability and make sure you are consistent with the laws, policies and procedures that you have studied. Make sure your answers are consistent with the position you are applying for, not just your current position. For example, if you are applying for a supervisory position and are asked a "what if . . ." question, you should answer it as if you are the supervisor, and not respond by saying: "I'd call the sergeant." The length of your responses will vary, of course, but be sure they fully answer the question. Stop when you are done.

Much like testifying in court, sometimes you can say too much. If the board wants more information, they will ask a follow-up question.

Expect questions on "hot topics" that have recently been in the news or that have recently affected your agency. These might include sexual harassment, employee drug use, discrimination, recent law changes and recent changes in your policies and procedures. Questions on any new material can often trip up an unprepared candidate.

When the interview is nearly over, they may ask you a catch-all question like: "Is there anything that you would like to ask the Board?"

Do what you want, but you should be confident that you have done your research and you should know what the job you are applying for requires, what it pays, etc., so there should be no reason to ask these types of questions. An appropriate response, in a confident voice, might be; "No sir. I think my research and preparation has given me insights into what the job requires and I am confident that I can meet those requirements if I am selected for the position." Before you leave the room, thank the board for the opportunity to be interviewed.

Here is one last tip on how to do well on oral boards. If you are already working in a criminal justice agency, make it known to your boss that you would like to sit on an oral board for new candidates applying for entry-level positions. Or ask around and maybe you can sit on an oral board in a neighboring criminal justice agency. If you are chosen to sit on the board, hopefully you will be trained what to look for in a candidate, what responses are more "right" than others, how candidates succeed or fail, and you will see first-hand how an oral board weighs a candidate's responses. Obviously, this training will do you well in preparing for *your* next promotional oral board interview.

Okay, that's our quick overview of oral boards. Now go get yourself an up-to-date book on how to take and perform well on oral boards, in-basket exercises or assessment centers. That type of book will provide you with practice exercises and much more detailed instructions than we can provide here. The bottom line on this entire chapter is that in order to be successful in a competitive environment, you must prepare better than your competition. Most people will not have the vision to look ahead, nor the motivation to prepare as well as you. That will give you a big edge over your competition, and will get you promoted ahead of your co-workers.

As a final example of what some of your competition is doing to try to take *your* next promotion, we leave you with a chance meeting we had with a person who we met on vacation with his family in a resort area. We met him fishing with his children on a sunny afternoon, and through a random conversation, we found that he was a sergeant in a criminal justice agency several hundred miles away. As he was packing up to leave, he casually mentioned that he had to go back to the motel and study for a couple of hours. Our curiosity got the better of us, and we inquired further. It turns out he was preparing to take a promotional test for lieutenant that was coming up. We asked him what he had done to prepare. We will quickly summarize his response.

He started preparing nine months before the test. He had taken a management course at a nearby college to brush up, he had spent about $500. buying all of the textbooks listed on the "book list" for the test, he had searched out a consultant who specialized in "how to get promoted" and went to a two-day seminar half-way across the country (by taking vacation days to do it), he had met with a successful private business contact to talk about what private business looks for in promoting managers, he had joined a local Toastmasters International to improve his speaking skills (which is where he met the business man mentioned previously), he had reviewed all his notes from a previous promotional exam he had taken (and done poorly on) and was working on his weaknesses, he had listed on his calendar how much time he was going to study each week, and what topics he was going to study, for the next four months. His plan was to study about fifteen hours a week (including his vacation week) for six months prior to the test. Sounds like a lot of work, doesn't it? It is! But . . . this is what some of your competition is doing.

"Those who prepare best, get promoted first," and you can quote us on that!

REVIEW QUESTIONS:

1. When is the best time to start preparing for your next promotional exam? Why?

2. What are five skills necessary to succeed on promotional exams that can be learned or improved on?

3. What are four ways of keeping up-to-date with policies, procedures and laws?

4. What are four tips to consider in preparing for an oral board interview?

5. Describe a workable and doable plan that you could follow in preparing for your next promotional exam?

CHAPTER 5

Role of the Supervisor—Part I

The next few chapters may be the most important for the long-term success of your career. This is where you will get the foundation principles of supervision and leadership. Consider these chapters as the building blocks upon which you will be able to build level after level of your criminal justice career just as builders make a strong foundation for a multi-story building. You will add additional levels throughout your career.

We recognize the diversity of the students who may be reading this book. You may be a newly appointed sergeant, or a 10-year veteran officer working for a city police department. You may be a corrections officer, in court security, or a parole/probation officer at some level. You may work for a rural sheriffs' department or a state police agency. Rest assured that it doesn't matter. The basic principles for being a successful supervisor, manager and leader, apply to any criminal justice agency. It's all about doing your job to the best of your ability, and taking care of your people.

Learning & Legitimization

Based on your past education, training and experience, you may be learning some of the following management terms, concepts, theories and practices for the first time. Or, you may feel that "I know that" in some of the segments. Good! Then this book may just simply legitimize what you are already doing and that means you are doing it right.

But, whatever your past education, training and experience have been, we hope this book will be of value to you in your career. We are confident that it will be. So let's get to the nuts and bolts of becoming successful in criminal justice supervision and leadership.

You will change

Just letting it be known that you are seeking a promotion may have a profound effect on you and others in your workplace. Some of your "friends" may back away from you a bit. Some others will be supportive of you, including some of your current supervisors. And, all that is *before* you get promoted. Then, once you get promoted to a supervisory position, things will really change for you and others. Yes, with the acceptance of those stripes or bars, you and your relationships will change in a variety of ways.

First, you are now a part of the "management team." You are no longer a line worker or first line officer. You are a manager. You are on the management team now because you are now aligned more with the sergeants, lieutenants, captains and majors than with line officers. Plus with this job change, you must recognize that your "peer group" has now changed. You are no longer "one of the guys" or "one of the girls." You are now a manager. You will quickly learn to leave the retirement parties earlier than you did as an officer, lest you witness something you don't want to be involved with, or lest an officer with a couple of drinks down wants to tell you what he REALLY thinks of your management skills.

There may be select individuals with whom you can maintain a "friends" style of relationship, but several of your past "friends" may shun you, or force you to adjust your relationship with them if they try to request special favors or treatment from you as their new supervisor. Handle friendships with line officers very carefully and professionally. Your true friends will understand, while your "pseudo-friends" will ask for inappropriate favors, ask that you cover up their mistakes, or throw the "I thought we were friends" in your face when you have to discipline them. These are not your true friends.

Your "Ten Responsibilities"

As a criminal justice supervisor, you are now responsible for many new things. Here are ten areas of responsibilities you must pay attention to if you are to be a successful supervisor in your organization.

1. *You are responsible for the performance of others.*

Somehow being a line officer will seem like it was easy work. You handled your basic duties and you did your paperwork. You were only responsible for your own actions. Now, however, you are responsible for the actions, antics, paperwork and follow-up of several employees; some better than others. But, whatever they do, you are responsible for them.

2. *You are responsible for the effective utilization of resources.*

That's kind of a fancy phrase for saying that you are responsible to have the right number of people, in the right place, at the right time, with the right equipment. That's true whether it's staffing a routine shift, or dealing with a riot situation.

3. *You are responsible for identifying and developing future supervisors.*

Identifying future supervisors is fairly easy. They look a lot like you. They show up early, handle their cases professionally, do their reports on time and seldom get complaints. Their arrest and conviction rates are high and they always look professional and well-groomed.

Developing these excellent employees into future supervisors requires some work on your part. It is your job to encourage them, get them the proper training for their future and "to take them under your wing;" not playing favorites, but developing a future leader. If you think back, perhaps someone took you under his or her wing. Now it's time to give back to others as well as the organization, by developing its future leaders.

4. *You are responsible for the training of your employees.*

"That's the Academy's responsibility," you say? Wrong!

The first line supervisor is responsible for the training of his or her personnel. Yes, the academy gave them some basics, but you must be sure they know and understand your organization's policies and procedures. This is particularly critical in the highest risk areas such as vehicle pursuits, use of force, sexual harassment prevention and a host of other areas.

Spend time with your people at roll call, or over coffee. But, be sure they are well-trained. If they complain about "Gee, Sarge, not the pursuit policy again," explain to them that it is for the good of everyone; them, you, the organization and the people you serve.

5. *You are responsible for implementing upper level decisions.*

Whether you agree or disagree with an upper level management decision, you are responsible for implementing that decision. If you disagree—tough! Take it up at the next management meeting. But, in the meantime, you will follow the concept of "unity of command." In short, that means that the "management team" speaks with one voice. That voice is yours, regardless of what level above you the decision was originally made.

In other words, you give the order. You don't say, "The Captain wants . . ." or "The Chief wants . . ." It is you who wants the action carried out. If anyone objects, they can see you, but the order is to be followed.

6. *You are responsible to act as a buffer between management and labor.*

Closely related to #5 above, you must take some heat from above, and some heat from below. Think of yourself wearing a bullet-resistant vest that absorbs grief and problems instead of a bullet. You will always wear that grief-absorbing vest as a supervisor.

The management people will often be in conflict with the labor people. You need to understand that the people on both sides of you have different agendas and pressures. It is up to you to reconcile any differences. You will absorb some of the energy from both sides, and you will continually be reconciling the issues as best you can for overall harmony in your workplace.

7. *You are responsible for maintaining the standards within your unit.*

These standards include discipline and safety standards. Most organizations have standard rules and regulations which employees are expected to follow. You are responsible for enforcing those rules and regulations even-handedly.

The enforcement of safety standards is a curious anomaly in any criminal justice agency. It's an inherently dangerous job, but your responsibility is to protect your people from unnecessarily high risks. The risks can come from outside sources, or from employees taking unnecessary risks on their own. In either case, only put your employees at risk when it is absolutely necessary.

8. *You are responsible for accurate record keeping.*

Yes, we know you didn't get into criminal justice work to do paperwork. Well, yes you did, because that is a part of criminal justice work. You can accept that as a supervisor, and you can carry that same message to anyone who complains about his or her own paperwork.

How important is record keeping? Try losing the paperwork on a couple of cases of ammunition that were delivered to your unit and you will quickly find out!

9. *You are responsible for fostering good inter-departmental relations.*

Police, fire, EMS, jails and courts all deal with the same calls, problems and people, but sometimes with different agendas. Those different agendas can sometimes result in conflicts between the line personnel of the various agencies. That's where you enter the scene.

All of those outside agencies will be working together for years to come, and they really need to work in harmony. Make it happen. Try to resolve any lingering conflicts with your peer in the other agency. If all else fails, go to your boss and let your boss resolve it with his or her peer in the other agency.

The same thing works with your own city, town, village or county agency personnel. Fostering harmony in all aspects of the workplace is a critical responsibility of yours.

10. *You are responsible for keeping yourself sane.*

Yes, the stresses placed on a criminal justice supervisor can be substantial. That's why you get paid the big bucks!

But, you can effectively handle those stresses by maintaining a sense of humor, no matter how bad things get. Also, be sure to stay as relaxed as you can. "This, too, shall pass," should be your motto when things get really hectic. Think about the police sergeant who was on duty when the planes hit the World Trade Center. Think about the police sergeant who was in charge of the shift in Oklahoma City when the federal building blew up. It's all tough stuff, but that's why you get paid the big bucks.

Handle the stress. Maintaining a positive attitude can help. Knowledge, training and experience can give you the confidence to handle any situation, thereby helping to manage the stress of any incident.

And that's it. Your "10 Most Wanted" responsibilities. And, your fun is just beginning. After your five review questions, we will move deeper into the realities of your job as a criminal justice supervisor.

REVIEW QUESTIONS:

1. If you are now on the "management team," who else is on the team?

2. Why has your peer group changed just because you got promoted?

3. Explain the term "effective utilization of resources" as it applies to the job of a criminal justice supervisor?

4. How would you handle the implementation of a decision from upper management when you thought it was wrong?

5. Why are safety standards a responsibility of a criminal justice supervisor?

CHAPTER 6

Role of the Supervisor—Part II

The job of a first line supervisor in any criminal justice agency can be one of the toughest. However, it can also be one of the most rewarding positions as you help other employees build their own careers. As the supervisor, you will be there to be a role model, and you will be there when they hit the highest points of their careers. You will also be there with your leadership skills to help them through their own "tough" times in their careers.

To be effective though, you must "understand" your job, including the competing pressures and influences that you will have to deal with to be successful in any agency. In this chapter, we will introduce you to a few of the influences and issues that can seriously affect your criminal justice career, if you are not properly prepared to deal with them.

Internal pressures

First, recognize that you will receive pressure from higher ranking administrators, as well as pressure from those lower in rank. Everyone has their own agendas that they want you to follow. The administration wants to cut costs, and the employees want to be paid as much as possible. Your employees want less paperwork, while the administration wants more documentation on each case. The conflicts are endless, and you are in the middle.

Well, then recognize that fact and handle it. The first step in handling these day-to-day conflicts is to recognize that they exist, and that they are part of your job. Then you need to deal with each conflict, issue by issue. You will gain compliance and concessions from each side. Consensus is nice when you can get it, but decision-making and implementation to the satisfaction of all is the leadership you need to exhibit during any conflict. You can do it.

Outside pressures

Closely related to the everyday internal skirmishes you must resolve is the problem of outside influences that will affect your work. You will face political influences on your work and the work of your people. Media influences may affect you in critical or high profile incidents. Then there is always the "L" word: liability, that can influence how you work.

Once you recognize that these influences exist, you are on the road to handling them effectively. Over time, you will learn to "do the right thing," in the face of outside influence. If you do what is *right,* you place the politician, the reporter or the lawyer in a position where they must defend why they think you should act contrary to "the right thing." Often they will just go away, perhaps badmouthing you or your agency, but they will go away. And you will be left, having done "the right thing."

Recognition—or not

As a supervisor, you will learn to notice, praise and reinforce the good work of the people under your own command. But, what happens if your good work as a supervisor is overlooked, and you aren't noticed, praised or reinforced? Oh, well, you know you are doing well. That knowledge, your own confidence and your paycheck should be enough to sustain you.

Management terms and issues

In order to be successful, you should also understand the meaning of several general management terms, the issues that surround them and how they can affect your career. You may have heard them in the past, and you may have your own definitions of them. But, we will cover them now, just to refresh your memory.

Chain of Command

Most criminal justice agencies have adopted a para-military command structure that parallels standard military ranks. Knowing who you report to and who the on-scene commander is at the scene of an incident, both by visual and verbal rank indicators, makes life easier for both the members of the criminal justice community and members of the public. In essence, they know who they are dealing with at any given time. Although name variations can occur between agencies and organizations, the general uniformed rank structure is:

Officer
Sergeant
Lieutenant
Captain
Major
Colonel
Chief or Director or Superintendent

The size of the organization generally dictates the rank structure and titles. Each rank needs to have input, and be kept informed by the rank immediately below them. Then, that rank can add information and report to the rank immediately above them. That is the concept of the chain of command. As a rule, do not bypass the chain of command. Although it may seem bureaucratic, following the chain of command can prevent many management problems. The consequences of not following the chain of command can include:

Unclear orders
No accountability
Missed communication
Lack of information by some ranks and, in the case of critical incidents, actual chaos can reign.

If you are bypassed in the chain of command, up or down the chain, you must address the issue so it does not occur in the future. Although each such incident has its own specific characteristics, there are some general guidelines to follow when addressing the issue of you having been bypassed.

1. *Be diplomatic*—Whether it was a subordinate or a boss that left you out of the chain, approaching them professionally will get the problem solved best.

2. *Be assertive*—Your position requires that you be in the chain of command to be an effective supervisor. Be sure you make that clear to others.

3. *Ask for future compliance*—A demanding style is not likely to be your best option. Asking the offending parties to be sure to "go through you" the next time is likely to garner the best results from the offending parties.

Unity of Command

This term is used to describe the fact that the "management team" speaks with one voice. To illustrate this point, suppose the chief of police signs an order that all police cars will be washed each shift. That order goes down through the chain of command and ends up on your desk as the new shift sergeant. You are to convey that order to your people as if it was your order.

There should be no "The Chief wants me to tell you..." or "The Lt. wants me to tell you . . ." No! It is *your* order. Where it originated from is not an issue. It is up to you to implement it, speaking with one management voice—yours.

Division of Labor

This term refers to the fact that everyone in the organization, at every rank, must do their job in order to be sure the overall mission of the organization gets done. The officers must properly handle all calls and cases, the sergeants must be sure they do, as well as check reports, effectively get people and equipment to scenes of incidents and ensure that the paperwork gets done. Lieutenants oversee a shift or unit to be sure all runs well, while the chief or sheriff deals with the politicians to get the money and resources necessary to run the department. Everyone in the organization has a job to do, and, if they do it, the overall job gets done for the community you serve. That is the Division of Labor concept.

Acceptance as a Supervisor

There are several groups of people who will be watching what you do as a new supervisor. These groups may or may not give you a "honeymoon" period to get your feet on the ground. But rest assured that they all will eventually pass judgment on you as a supervisor. Naturally, you will want to be accepted as a legitimate supervisor, but it's not that easy. Here are some of the groups who are watching you and how you should handle them.

Subordinates: Leadership is action, not just position. Just because you have the stripes or bars doesn't mean you are in charge. As a new supervisor, those who work under your command want to be sure that you know what to do and how to do it. They want to be sure you won't needlessly endanger them, either on the street or administratively. Show them that you know what to do and then do it, not arrogantly, but professionally and legitimately.

Supervisors: Your bosses already have faith in you because they have given you the bars or stripes. Therefore, their support is generally yours to lose. They need a good supervisor and they will try to support you where they can. So, if you do your job right, you will have their support. Even if you make an occasional mistake, they will help you fix it. Make too many mistakes and you can lose their support.

Peers: You could be working with the supervisors of several other units, both inside and outside your agency. Whether it is the detectives, SWAT, or EMS or Fire, they will be interacting with you and your unit, and judging your abilities as a supervisor. To gain their acceptance, do your job. If you know what you are doing, they will recognize that fact. Your reputation, good or bad, will have often preceded you through your subordinates' answers to, "So how's that new boss of yours working out?"

Resolve any conflicts between units with your peer in that affected unit. If EMS is trampling your crime scenes, go to their shift supervisor, professionally and diplomatically, to try to come to a common understanding. If you can't resolve the problem, over time, then it is time to ask your boss to resolve the problem with his/her peer.

Competition from peers

Within your own department, you may find competition from some of your peers. After all, you are in competition for the next higher rank, and, it is only human nature to protect one's own "turf."

Once again, act professionally and diplomatically to resolve any conflicts. But, be sure to protect yourself, your unit and your people at all times. If you can't resolve a problem over time with your peer, then ask advice or action from your boss, citing all the efforts you have put forth to resolve the problem over time.

The best option for being successful as a criminal justice supervisor at any rank is to know what you are doing and do it. If you work hard and have the education, training, and experience for your position, others will recognize you as a professional who knows what they are doing. Once they encounter you, they will want to have you as an ally, not an enemy. You will then deal from a position of strength. Your reputation as a good commander will have preceded you. There will still be some minor conflicts, but you will have gained a reputation that will make others want to settle any conflicts with you, quickly.

REVIEW QUESTIONS

1. Name two outside influences that can affect your job as a criminal justice supervisor.

2. Explain the term "chain of command."

3. What action should you take if someone bypasses you in the chain of command?

4. Explain the concept of "division of labor" as it relates to you as a criminal justice supervisor.

5. Name three groups who will be watching your performance as a new supervisor.

CHAPTER 7

Management Styles and Theories—Part I

Does one style of leadership work all the time?

Well, first you have to know what styles of leadership there are before you can answer that question. In the next two chapters, you will learn about the basic styles of leadership. We have greatly simplified the theories and studies and broken them into some of their basic elements to give you a very brief overview of them. After being exposed to the various styles of leadership, and the results of past studies of successful leaders, you will be better equipped to answer the question above. You will also be better prepared to start to develop your own style of leadership for the future, partially based on what you learn here.

Autocratic or democratic

The autocratic style of leadership is, in essence, "Do it because I said so." This style is demanding and commands immediate obedience to the order of the commander. On the other end of the spectrum is the democratic style of leadership. In essence, this leadership style solicits input from the unit members regarding the solving of problems and the decision making process. The "decision" is made by the group, with the approval of the supervisor.

To illustrate the contrast between the two leadership styles, envision two problems that might confront a police commander. The first is a hostage situation involving an armed man holding several people hostage and threatening to kill one each hour until his demands are met. The second situation involves where and how to get the patrol cars washed on a daily basis. These two situations are clearly different and the handling of them can be placed on opposite ends of the autocratic/democratic spectrum.

As our hostage-taker screams obscenities at the police and exhibits clearly unstable behavior, a police commander has no time to have his people "vote" on any police actions to be taken. The commander must take command and, if required, autocratically authorize a green light for the sniper to neutralize the hostage-taker, before the hostage-taker can take a life. In doing so, the commander has exhibited an autocratic leadership style. This is not bad, and under the circumstances, is an acceptable and necessary means of handling the situation

In sharp contrast, how the cars get washed has neither a critical component, nor a severe time constraint. Nobody is likely to die over this type of decision. Therefore, a "vote" or at least input from those who will actually be getting the cars washed, can work for the police supervisor. Reaching a consensus among members exhibits a democratic style of leadership.

Most of the time, you will operate on a sliding scale, mostly toward the middle of the two extremes of the spectrum given in the examples. Your personality may sway you one direction or another, but that's okay. You must lead consistent with your own personality, whether it leans toward autocratic or democratic.

McGregor's Theory X and Theory Y

A fellow named Douglas McGregor studied managers and came to the conclusion that managers' actions generally fall within the two major categories of management theory which he termed "Theory X" and "Theory Y."

The Theory X manager believes the following premises:

1. The average human being has an inherent dislike of work and will avoid it if he can.

2. Most people must be coerced, controlled, directed and threatened with punishment to get them to put forth adequate effort.

3. The average human being prefers to be directed, wants to avoid responsibility, has relatively little ambition and wants security above all.

The Theory Y manager believes in quite the opposite premises:

1. The expenditure of physical and mental effort in work is as natural as play or rest.
2. Man will exercise self-direction and self-control in the service of objectives to which he is committed.
3. The capacity to exercise a high degree of imagination, ingenuity, and creativity to solve organizational problems is widely, not narrowly, distributed in the population.

Clearly, Theory X and Theory Y represent two diverse management views of the workforce. What is your view of the employees who work for you?

Trait theories of leadership

There have been repeated efforts to try to identify what makes a successful leader. These studies focused on the traits of the leaders themselves. We present some of the findings of these studies here, once again, broken down into some of their simplest elements.

Physical traits: At least one study of the chief executive officers of Fortune 500 companies found that they were overwhelmingly male, over six feet tall and "big" people. That's nice and may support the "command presence" theory of people who look like they're in charge, but that theory is not conclusive. Napoleon and Hitler, both of whom nearly took over the world, were both relatively small-statured people. And, Mahatma Gandhi, the one-time leader of India was certainly a small statured person after his many hunger strikes. Stature may be one element of successful leadership, but there are many other traits that have been identified that have more widespread credibility. Here are some of the other common traits of successful leaders.

Intelligence: Successful leaders have an intelligence level that is slightly higher than their peers, but not necessarily a great deal higher. Intelligence is required in successful leaders so that they can have the analytical skills to see broad problems and complicated relationships. Intelligence is also required for effective communication skills. A leader must be able to communicate their ideas, directives and orders both orally and in writing. They also must be able to understand their people in order to motivate them. And, they must be intelligent enough to understand what others are communicating to them from above or below.

Social Maturity and Breadth: Successful leaders have broad interests and indulge in a variety of activities. The whole world fascinates them. They seek out information and understanding on a wide variety of topics. That is in contrast to the more "technical" types of personalities who tend to focus on a very narrow area of interest. We need both types of people, but leaders tend to be the more diverse of the two.

Leaders also tend to be more emotionally mature. They are neither crushed by defeat nor over-elated by winning. Leaders also tend to have a high frustration tolerance. They also have minimal anti-social attitudes such as hostility to others who don't agree with them, or who are different. In general, they treat everyone with dignity and respect.

Leaders also have reasonable self-assurance and self-respect. These traits come naturally to those who have worked hard to get the education, training and experience for their position. They know that they know, and others sense their confidence and ability and respect them for it.

Inner Motivation: Leaders have a strong personal motivation toward personal accomplishment. As one goal is reached, they aspire to another. They work more for self-satisfaction than for external rewards. Many criminal justice executives don't even know how much money they make, providing the pay in their organization is adequate for their needs.

They also accept responsibility for themselves, their unit and their people. Responsibility is the vehicle that gives them the opportunity to achieve. They are risk-takers. They can afford to take risks because they know their roles, their jobs and they have the confidence that they will make the right decisions.

Understanding People: Leaders understand that people are the key to their success. Little is done in criminal justice without key people in key places from the line officer to the head of the agency. Successful leaders approach specific problems in terms of the people involved; their strengths, weaknesses and their mission. The most successful leaders are employee-oriented. They preserve and develop human dignity among their people.

Preparation: As Abraham Lincoln said even before he was a candidate for president, "I will prepare and my time will come."

Leaders prepare for success. They develop social understanding and appropriate skills. They learn how to shake hands with both men and women. They learn to make eye contact with both friends and foes. They learn to smile appropriately. They develop manners for all social and professional occasions. Whether it is taking the appropriate actions at the Pledge of Allegiance to the flag or making small talk at a political gathering, they have learned the proper way to handle themselves

As you can see, most of the skills involved in becoming a successful leader can be learned. Then, it is just a matter of maximizing your strengths and minimizing your weaknesses while always trying to improve yourself in your weakest areas.

And last, successful leadership is an attitude: An attitude that you have properly studied and prepared, and that you are constantly doing your best for yourself, your people and the ideals of your agency. Do so, and your efforts will be recognized by your supervisors, your subordinates, your peers and the public.

REVIEW QUESTIONS:

1. Does one style of leadership work all the time? Explain your answer.

2. What are the primary differences between McGregor's Theory X and Theory Y premises?

3. What role does intelligence play in successful leadership and why?

4. Define in general terms, social maturity and breadth.

5. Why are the most successful leaders employee-oriented?

CHAPTER 8

Management Styles and Theories—Part II

The history of modern management is relatively new. Until the Industrial Revolution farmers, artisans and tradesmen dominated American culture, often working alone or in small groups. With the advent of the Industrial Revolution, production of products became much more complex, requiring larger and larger groups of people to accomplish ever more complex tasks. The development of the assembly line style of manufacturing required an "overseer" [manager] to be sure that manpower and parts all came together efficiently to put out quality manufactured goods at affordable prices.

Over the next 100 years, people began to study the management process in American plants and industries to get maximum effectiveness and efficiency. The synopsis that follows provides a very brief look at a few of the research studies, and draws some conclusions and lessons learned about workers and their managers. The results of these past studies are presented to help you understand what makes up and motivates the workforce in general, and the members of your agency in particular. Learn from them what you can on the way to developing your own style of management and leadership.

> "Those who would ignore the past are condemned to repeat it."

Frederick Taylor—Scientific Management

Frederick Taylor was perhaps the first efficiency expert to arrive on the American business scene. He studied "how" people worked and then analyzed this data to see how he could make workers most productive. In one study, he analyzed how workers shoveled coal. There had been wide disparities in the amounts of coal that individual workers could shovel in a day. Taylor studied the matter. He compared the productivity of individuals when they used long-handled vs. short-handled shovels. He ran tests changing the size of the shovel pan, half-full vs. full and a variety of other factors to find the most efficient combination to recommend for uniform productivity which could assure a particular level of productivity, day after day. So what does shoveling coal have to do with you as a supervisor in criminal justice?

Well, thanks to Taylor, for the first time, management and workers were brought together to talk. Management studied and defined the work and then they taught the workers to work efficiently. Once trained how to do their jobs and what was expected from them, the employees performed much better. Productivity for both was assured by this consistent method of working. With a guaranteed level of productivity, management could plan ahead with medium and long-term goals. The workers also benefited because they made more money for their increased efficiency. The bottom line of this research was that if the bosses and the workers talk about common goals, and the workers are taught what to do, how to do it, when to do it and why they are doing it . . . employees perform better. Seems way too simple, but is that being done in your agency?

Michigan Leadership Studies

Katz and Kahn conducted three major studies in the early 1950's. They studied high-producing and low-producing supervisors. From their studies, they found three variables of leadership behavior that were consistently related to the satisfactory productivity of work groups.

1. Successful leaders assume the leadership role. They plan, they delegate and they think and act like a supervisor. They recognized that they could no longer be "one of the guys." Some bosses in criminal justice are afraid to assume the role of the leader. It takes more than a boss yelling: "I'm the boss," to make them a leader.

2. When they examined the closeness of supervision, they found that high production supervisors did not supervise as closely as low production supervisors. They concluded that people need a degree of freedom in order to do their jobs. This goes back to 'Theory Y' from the previous chapter. Good bosses trust their employees, they encourage them, they give them room to grow.

3. The study found that top supervisors are employee-oriented. They have concern for the workers as individuals. Good supervisors take an interest in promoting the welfare of the workers. And, good supervisors learn to motivate their employees to be good workers. Good bosses get to know their employees as people, not just as workers. All of us, bosses and employees, have certain 'needs'. One of these basic needs is the need to be appreciated. Good bosses learn how to do that for all their employees. This is important because all your employees have this need—the outstanding ones, the average employees and the marginal performers. Are you doing your part for all your employees, or do you tend to encourage and appreciate only your better employees?

Ohio State Studies

The Ohio State Studies identified six attributes of successful leaders:

1. The leader finds time to listen to employees.
2. The leader is willing to make changes.
3. The leader is friendly and approachable.
4. The leader assigns employees to particular tasks.
5. The leader asks employees to follow standard rules and regulations in the workplace.
6. The leader lets employees know what is expected of them.

These seem so simple, but how many bosses have you worked for over the years that were missing some (or all) of these attributes?

Hawthorne Studies

This series of studies focused on employee behaviors. Here are some of their findings:

1. Employees liked having someone interested in studying their work. They felt someone cared about them. (Sounds like a combination of "Theory Y" and the "Michigan State Study.")

2. Employees want to talk with their supervisors, at least on occasion. (Sounds like a combination of the "Michigan State Study" and the "Ohio State Study.")

3. Employees build up strong personal bonds with their co-workers. (More proof that most of these studies find only a few differences between "bad bosses" and "good bosses," but these few differences are critical!)

4. Workers have a distrust of management. They feel that management will always want more from them. Therefore, they tend to set up informal quotas for a day's productivity, and they work only to reach that informal quota. (Sounds like the "Taylor Study.")

Blake & Mouton

These researchers found that managers must balance their concern for getting the job done versus the amount of concern they have for their workers. They developed a detailed survey, which, once completed and scored, is plotted on a Managerial Grid to show the degree of concern for people versus the concern for tasks that a manager must accomplish. In short, the manager must balance the concern for the task at hand (the mission), and the concern for his people.

As a criminal justice example, let's say that one of your people is getting married on Saturday and she wants your whole unit, including you, to be there at the wedding. Yet, you have a commitment to be sure that your unit has adequate staffing on the job at the same time. How would you balance that?

Situational Leadership

This is a leadership model developed by two researchers named Blanchard and Hersey in the 1970s. Its basic advice for supervisors is to "treat what you see." Their model allows the supervisor to evaluate an individual's knowledge and maturity level, and then decide as to the course of action best suited to motivating the individual employee.

Although a bit complicated and requiring at least two days of training to fully understand the model, two conclusions are readily apparent.

1. Leave your best people alone to do their jobs. Pat them on the back occasionally, but essentially leave them alone.

2. For employees who don't know how to do the job or who are unwilling to do the job, you must, figuratively, lead them along through each step of the job, until such time as they reach the next maturity level of being more willing and more able to do the job.

Each employee is an individual, with different levels of ability, motivation, knowledge, training, etc. A good supervisor knows each employee and adjusts to the needs, motivation, etc. of each employee. Basically, the supervisor changes his/her tactics according to each employee. It is difficult to do, yet we all want to be treated as individuals.

This has been a very fast and limited review of the history of managerial studies, styles and theories. There is no time here to provide any more details. Just take what you have read, answer the review questions and glean what you can from the findings to add to your choices for your own "managerial style." After all, your career depends on it.

REVIEW QUESTIONS

1. What was Frederick Taylor's contribution to the body of information about workers and management?

2. What is likely to be the effect of the closeness of supervision on employee productivity and morale?

3. Many of the studies found that the best supervisors are employee-oriented. Why do you think that the findings are valid?

4. Why would workers set informal production quotas? What might you do to change their minds?

5. At least two of the studies found that management should let employees know what is expected of them. Why?

CHAPTER 9

Leadership Skills—Part I

There are many different ways to look at leadership. Lots of books have been written on this topic. There are millions of web pages to look at on the Internet if you want to learn more about leadership. But, let's try to keep it simple: *"A leader is one who knows the way, goes the way and shows the way."* (John C. Maxwell) Let's take this definition apart and examine it more closely in this chapter.

This is as simple, yet as complex, a definition of leadership as you may ever see. It sounds so simple. But, if it were that simple, why isn't the world (and the field of criminal justice in particular) full of great leaders?

Well, there are only three simple parts of this definition. Yet, these may be the same three things that are missing from too many bosses in the field of criminal justice.

If you are going to be successful in the field of criminal justice, you will at some point have to assume the role of being a leader. Long before that happens, you should be preparing yourself to assume a leadership role. This chapter will review some of the issues involved in understanding what it takes to become a leader, and what you can do to develop the traits and attributes that may help you assume a leadership role.

"A leader is one who knows the way . . ."

We hate to use an over-used phrase, but, here goes . . . leaders see the "big picture." One valuable trait of leaders is that they have a lot of knowledge about a lot of different aspects of their criminal justice agency. They know the right thing to do, and they know how this will affect other people and other agencies. These people know the importance of understanding how all aspects of their job work, and how the interactions of their job relates to the interactions of the rest of the criminal justice system, the political world, the community, the media, etc.

Of course, being a leader is a lot more than being called "The Boss." There are too many people in positions of power who are not leaders. And, conversely, there are people who have no special title or rank or position who are recognized by their peers and bosses as being a leader. Leadership is funny . . . some people who are in a powerful position or have a title to be leaders aren't, and yet some people with no title or position are.

". . . goes the way . . ."

Have you ever worked for a boss that you really admired?
Have you ever worked for a boss that you really trusted?
Have you ever worked for a boss that you really respected?
What made this boss different from the other bosses that you've worked for? We suggest that you write down on a piece of paper the five traits that make "good bosses" good, and then list the five traits the make "bad bosses" bad. Later on in this chapter, we will list some of these, but we want you to make up your own list.

It is more than a coincidence that "good bosses" have employees who are motivated, who get the job done right, who have a low number of complaints, low use of sick leave, and their employees seem to enjoy coming to work. Good bosses have employees who are motivated, seem to enjoy their work and always get the job done. Bad bosses . . . no fun to work for!

Here are a couple of questions for you to think about: Are you a leader? Do you have the traits and characteristics that people associate with leadership? Do your peers or superiors think you are a leader? This is important, so take a few minutes to think about these questions and be honest in your answers.

There are many different studies done on the topic of leadership, and the bookstores are full of books on this topic. You should do some homework on this topic, as we believe it is one of the defining traits of successful criminal justice professionals.

". . . and shows the way."

One of the most common phrases in discussing leadership is: *"Lead by example."* Whether you are a commander in a large police department, a 15-year probation officer, or a new employee just hired in a criminal justice agency, this should become your motto if you want to succeed in criminal justice.

As you well know, there are formal leaders and informal leaders in any criminal justice agency. You should strive to become one of them. You do not become a leader automatically because you get promoted. Leadership is earned by the consensus of your peers or bosses. People agree that you are a leader. They feel comfortable giving you that position, and they feel comfortable following your direction.

Think about the word *leadership*. A current management expert (John Maxwell) sums up the definition of leadership as " . . . influence—nothing more, nothing less." This means that you must be able to influence other people. It also means that leadership is built on what people think of you—your character, your integrity, your work ethic, your decision making abilities, your trustworthiness. This is how you influence others to *follow* you. This is how you *lead* people.

Leadership traits

A survey of 600 criminal justice supervisors was taken to determine what they thought were the most positive and the most negative leadership traits. The results appear below. Review both lists and learn from them.

Most Positive Leadership Traits
1. Has Good Common Sense
2. Takes Command
3. Honesty/Integrity
4. Fair
5. Willing to Help
6. Consistent

Most Negative Leadership Traits
1. Close-Minded
2. Two-Faced
3. Arrogant/Egotistical
4. Abuses Power
5. Inconsistent
6. Holds a Grudge
7. Indecisive

Characteristics of Leaders

Our experience is that leadership is lacking in some criminal justice agencies. Too many bosses believe they are leaders because of their title or the position that they hold, but only a select few have earned the title of "leader." What is it that sets "leaders" apart from their peers? Here is a list of a few of the personal attributes a criminal justice "leader" should possess:

Honesty

In repeated surveys, honesty is listed as the *number one* attribute subordinates want in a leader.

Courage

Both physical and moral courage are necessary to be a successful leader. The physical courage is necessary to be able to face crisis situations in a calm and efficient manner. Moral courage is necessary to face adversity, stand up for your people and to handle mistakes and problems. Both physical and moral courage are necessary to be able to "stand up" to superior officers, adversity and personal criticism.

Dependability

A leader is someone who can always be depended on to keep his/her word and show up on time, and to do whatever is needed to accomplish the task at hand.

Optimism

A leader is a positive person. They tend to focus on the positive aspects of a situation rather than the negatives of the same situation. That positive attitude is uplifting to their subordinates and inspires them to also look on the positive side of the situation.

Creativity

Since leaders think in terms of solutions, not problems, they are more likely to find creative solutions to problems that would demoralize and stymie others.

Confidence

Leaders know that they know. They have prepared themselves with all of the education, training and experience they could obtain. Now, they are confident in their own abilities.

Personal Energy

Successful leaders have an inner personal energy that allows them to think and move quickly and with an enthusiasm that is infectious to all who work with them.

Loyalty

Leaders are loyal to their organization, their bosses, their subordinates and themselves. These loyalties are long-term commitments. Such loyalty is always rewarded through reciprocity, adding to the leader's and unit's success.

Tact

Because leaders think before they say or act, they're seen as having tact in their interactions with everyone in their workplace. As a result, they don't hurt others' feelings or judge others rashly.

Humility

Leaders are humble. When the accolades start to flow for a job well done, they point to their subordinates and say, "They did it." Although leaders have strong egos, they keep them under control.

Time for you to think a little. Look again at that list of positive and negative leadership traits on the previous pages. Do you have the traits that are necessary to become a leader? Be honest!

But, here is another equally important question for you to consider. We are convinced that every bad boss that is out there *thinks* that he is a good boss, but their employees know differently. No matter how good a leader you think you are, if your employees *think* that you are a bad boss, they will respond accordingly.

Leadership is a difficult position to achieve. It is a complex and ever-demanding personal challenge in any industry, but it is particularly challenging in the demanding field of criminal justice. Therefore, it is necessary to prepare yourself for the challenge of leadership. These ten traits are a beginning. Watch for further guidance in subsequent chapters of this book.

REVIEW QUESTIONS:

1. Define "vision" as it relates to leadership.

2. Why is it necessary for a leader to share their "vision"?

3. What is the number one attribute subordinates want in a leader?

4. Why is it necessary for a leader to possess both physical and moral courage?

5. How does a leader develop confidence in his/her ability?

CHAPTER 10

Leadership Skills—Part II

In the previous chapter, we talked about some of the characteristics and traits that good leaders have. Hopefully, you took an honest self-evaluation of who you are, what you do, and how you do it, and compared this to those leadership characteristics. This could be really important for your future, so take a few minutes to review the last chapter.

Supervisory training

One of the biggest obstacles to a successful career in criminal justice is the lack of consistent and mandatory training for new supervisors. Some agencies have a lot of supervisory training, some agencies have a little training and some agencies have no training. Some states mandate training for some criminal justice supervisors, but not for others. If training is done, it is often a minimum of what *should* be done. (Most of the states in the country do not mandate *any* police supervisory training.) So, without mandatory supervisory training, or with inconsistent supervisory training between various agencies and jurisdictions, what choices to you have to survive and succeed in the challenging field of criminal justice?

When you get promoted, your agency may decide not to train you, or to under-train you, in your new role as a supervisor. Yet, you are still responsible and accountable to perform to the highest standards possible, both for the good of your agency and for the good of your career. You will be placed in a very critical position in your agency, and you cannot afford to make too many mistakes. Now you have choices, of course; you can sit back with minimal supervisory training and hope you don't make too many mistakes and don't get into too much trouble, or, you can take charge of your own career and try to gain the necessary supervisory and leadership skills on your own. Here are some options for you to consider to develop these necessary skills, if your agency under-trains you:

1. Enroll in a leadership or administration course at your local college. If your local college does not have a criminal justice degree, then many of the concepts taught in a business administration or organizational development course can be carried over into your job. And, some of your agencies will pay your tuition.

   Of course, there are many reputable colleges across the country that offer criminal justice administration degrees on-line. (There really aren't any good excuses for you not to go to college!)

2. Join a professional association that focuses on supervisory/management/leadership. Every field in criminal justice offers several of these. You will receive journals every month, updates on specific training and other benefits that can improve your leadership skills.

3. If you don't want to join a professional organization, then at least subscribe to a journal that focuses on criminal justice management. You have a choice, depending on what field of criminal justice you are involved in. Several of these are available on-line for **free!**

4. If you have any large corporations or businesses in your area, see if they are sponsoring any supervisory/leadership training that you could attend. Many of the concepts will easily relate to your job.

We strongly believe that taking this initiative will improve your chances for a successful career for several very valid reasons. You will be glad you took this advice when you have to testify in court about your role as a supervisor, and the lawyer asks you: "What have you done to prepare yourself for the role of being a supervisor?" If you are making an effort to learn supervisory/leadership skills beyond what your agency does for you, it can only improve your career.

A word about loyalty

One of the guiding principles of being an effective leader is loyalty. The people who *let* you be a leader (remember, your leadership ability depends entirely on them letting you be a leader), expect something in return. One of the things that most people expect from their leaders is loyalty. Let's look at some ways of developing loyalty from your subordinates.

1. Be pleasant—Some leaders can be gruff and aloof, but . . . learn to develop a positive, outgoing and friendly attitude. You will usually get a lot more from your employees.

2. Know your people—Remember that your most valuable resource is the people who work for you. They are individuals, not objects. They have families, problems, feelings, good days and bad days. Learn their strengths and weaknesses and let them use their talents whenever possible. Let them try.

3. Help your people do their job—Make their job easier, not harder! You can either reduce obstacles that are in their way or block them further. Act as a buffer whenever possible. Make sure they have the right equipment and the right training to do their jobs.

4. Train your people—Do you assume that all your employees have equal training and have equal abilities to do their jobs? You know what happens when you "assume?" Do you encourage or discourage them? Do you tell them about upcoming training seminars, or share professional journals or kept them current with new technology?

5. Develop your employees—What about the goals of your employees? Do you know what they are, or do they think you don't care enough about them to ask? What skills does each of your employees have? How can these skills benefit your agency or your other employees?

6. Watch out for your people—Protect them as much as possible. Minimize the effects of their mistakes and magnify the effects of their accomplishments. Take care of

them—as long as they do not compromise your job or your career.

7. Maintain standards—Make sure they have all the resources they need to do their job. Make sure they know how to use the equipment that you have in your agency. Enforce your agency's policies reasonably, and let all of them know that you have high expectations of yourself and of them.

8. Be understanding—Each of your employees has problems, families, ups and downs. Understand that. Listen to them. Be willing to work through the ups and downs of their career (as long as they do not abuse this understanding).

The importance of loyalty cannot be underestimated. Loyalty and trust from your employees can go far in helping their career and yours. As you go higher in your organization, the people above you will recognize your value, and the employees who work for you will learn by your example how important loyalty is.

The ability to lead is an incredibly valuable skill that many criminal justice employees seek, but only a few achieve. But, contrary to an old saying ("Leaders are born, not made"), we believe that any person can develop and improve their leadership skills. Obviously some people will have more leadership talents and skills than others, but, as with many skills in life, the more you practice, the better you will get.

REVIEW QUESTIONS:

1. Why is supervisory/leadership training lacking in some criminal justice agencies?

2. What are four ways that you can develop supervisory skills beyond what your agency may give you?

3. Describe at least five ways that you can instill loyalty in your employees?

4. Why is loyalty an important leadership trait?

CHAPTER 11

Supervisory Response to Critical Incidents—Part I

As a criminal justice supervisor, much of your time will be spent on routine matters. You will attend meetings, review and write reports, and supervise the daily actions of your people. And then, without warning, chaos erupts in your quiet workplace.

Suddenly, you find yourself and your people in a situation that may involve blood, bullets, bodies or other critical, and potentially career-threatening problems. And, all of these problems, regardless of who started them, suddenly all belong to you! You are the person in charge and you must take action, but it must be the *right* action. These types of critical situations are what will define you as a mere manager or a true leader. And, it's all up to you—starting now!

Preparation

Most criminal justice agencies test promotional candidates on the material contained in local, state and/or federal laws, as well as the policy and procedure manual of the agency. Agencies want their supervisors to act within the law on all routine and unusual incidents. The policies and procedures of the agency have generally been well thought out and carefully written, and have likely been tested through experience and case law decisions. They are meant to provide supervisors with guidance on how to handle specific instances like injuries to personnel, use-of-force incidents, arrest situations and many other events that may occur in a criminal justice agency.

Therefore, if you are going to be in the position of a supervisor, you should be prepared by knowing the law and your policies and procedures; not just for the exam, but to help yourself and your people survive a critical incident. And, know them well! In the heat of a chaotic situation, amid screaming people, ambulances and perhaps inexperienced employees under your command, it's a little too late to start thumbing through your policy manual to figure out what you should be doing.

But, the preparation phase doesn't stop just with you knowing what to do and when to do it. Your people need to know what their duties and responsibilities are long before they get themselves in a bad situation. It is up to you to be sure that they also know the general laws and agency policies that apply to particular situations. Whether you go over policies routinely at the start of your shift or conduct formal training programs, the time for your people to learn is *before* an incident happens. In reality, many critical incidents can be prevented, or prevented from getting worse, by your employees following established policies and procedures in carrying out their duties.

Make a special effort to be sure both you and your people are well-versed in the laws, policies and procedures of your agency as they relate to critical, and possibly high-liability areas. These can include the use of force, injuries to people in custody, laws of arrest, search and seizure and pursuit of a vehicle. Other critical areas can include civil unrest, civil rights issues, and incidents involving the conduct of your people, both on duty and off duty.

Supervisory response

In your role as a supervisor, if you hear something unusual happening outside your office, on the radio, or out on the street, go investigate. Your mere presence may help to quell a difficult situation. At times, a quick decision from a knowledgeable supervisor can prevent an officer from acting improperly or help him/her make the right decision.

In any critical incident, if you think you should probably respond, then do it! And, let your people at the scene know you are on the way. Knowing you are responding may help control the situation at the scene. When civilians and agency personnel alike know that a supervisor is "on the way," it can help to defuse a potential problem. Your personal response can be considered as your way of getting out of the office to help, rather than hiding behind your desk while others do the "dirty work" out on the street.

Leadership

Getting to a critical incident is good, but once there, you must take charge. That means you must know what you are doing, and (equally important) you must show that you know. Ask questions, gather as much information as quickly as possible, direct others to help you control the scene. That might include such tasks as controlling the scene, setting up a perimeter, interviewing witnesses. Although you could do any one of these tasks, this is one of those times when you do not want to get too involved with these routine tasks. Your role is to direct, oversee the situation and be free to make decisions.

Trust us on this one. As a supervisor, you may be a mild annoyance to some of your people, but, when everything is in chaos, and they know that things are going to get bad, they want your leadership. So, give it to them by doing the right thing at every turn. Use every bit of the education, training and experience you have to solve their problem, before it becomes **your** problem!

Safety

In many critical incidents, the safety of your people and civilians alike is your responsibility. Whether it is a hostage situation, an inmate that refuses to leave his cell or a search warrant gone bad, safety is your primary issue.

Take the necessary precautions to make safety a top priority, whether you decide to evacuate an area, call for additional support or just make sure that your employees are kept out of harm's way. And, that includes your own safety as well. An injured supervisor will only make the situation worse.

Follow policies and procedures

You have spent all that time learning about laws, policies and procedures and now is the time to use that knowledge. Gather information, take charge of the situation and make the proper supervisory notifications consistent with your policies and procedures.

Now, we have mentioned that before, but here are a couple of questions that you need to answer now before it is too late. Where is your manual? Is it current with all of the latest updates? Are you *very* familiar with the high-liability incidents that could get you and your officers in the most trouble? Are your employee's manuals current and do they keep them handy? Are they familiar with their duties in the typical high-liability areas that could get them in the most trouble? This is a critical part of your job!

Document, document, document!

Whether it is remembering who enters a hazardous material spill incident, or who finds an article of evidence, you need to see that a log is maintained at any critical incident. This should include the time, action, personnel involved, and all actions that are taken. Whether or not this is required through your agency's policies or not, it makes good sense to maintain one to document the events, times and actions taken at the scene.

An example of a log entry might be:

> 12:47 pm—requested dispatch to notify hostage negotiations team and send to the scene.
>
> 12:56 pm—crime scene technicians arrived. Held back due to insecure area.
>
> 12:58 pm—directed Officers Jones, Smith and Richardson to evacuate adjacent buildings.

You get the idea. Most of these notes should end up in your final report, and could be invaluable if a civil litigation lawsuit is filed against you four months after the incident.

None of us like to do any more paperwork than necessary, but sometimes even the most routine matter deserves a report. Of course, you'll write a report on the fatal accidents and the injuries to prisoners and the use of force incidents, but don't overlook the minor day-to-day activities that you deal with routinely. A minor incident like an irate motorist that complains to you about the "rude" officer who just gave him a speeding ticket may not require a report, but this is the kind of routine matter that could come back to "bite you" if you don't document it.

Follow up on everything

It is not enough just to direct that action be taken. You must follow up on every action to be sure that it has been done. You may have directed an ambulance crew to take an injured officer to the small, local hospital, but they were directed by emergency room personnel to take him to a trauma center in a nearby city. You need to know that.

Continually check to be sure that necessary actions have been taken and that necessary notifications have been made. Continually check to see that all actions taken are consistent with existing policies and procedures of your agency.

Get help as needed

Few agencies have all the necessary resources to handle every type of critical incident. Probation and parole agencies do not usually have the crime scene expertise to handle an officer-involved shooting. Of course, you would call in the county sheriff or state police, but do you know the name of the supervisor or commander in those agencies on a first-name basis? It would be nice to know because it could facilitate inter-agency operations.

If you need a K-9 unit or helicopter or all-terrain vehicle or a blood spatter expert, do not hesitate to get one to the scene from another agency. Don't think you can handle everything, and don't be so stubborn that you would not call another agency if they can help you in a crisis. Read and follow your agency's mutual aid plan. If you don't know where it is, ask. Find it, read it in advance, and follow it when you need it.

Write the report—now!

Get your report done as soon as possible after the incident. Not only will everything be fresh in your mind, but you will be able to interpret your own notes better than if you wait. Of course, you should comply with all agency deadlines, but you could also get it done before those deadlines.

Get these things done now because there is another critical incident right behind this one. It's only a matter of time.

Debrief and learn

Critical incidents are not designed to run smoothly. If they did, they wouldn't be "critical"—they would be "routine." So, take the common sense approach, and examine what went right and what went wrong. Often this is done in a general meeting of all personnel involved. Sometimes neutral officers who were not involved in the incident (maybe even from another agency) will debrief everyone individually and will submit their findings to management.

The important things to examine are how could the incident have been prevented or limited. Are your current policies and procedures adequate to cover this type of incident? Was there adequate training? Was there adequate supervision? Was the right equipment available? What could have been done better? It is not enough just to ask these kinds of questions—action must be taken to make the next incident less critical.

Post incident trauma

Serious incidents can have serious psychological consequences for some of your personnel (and for you, too). Most often this post incident trauma occurs after officers are involved in a fatal use-of-force or a traffic accident involving serious injury or death. (Of course it can also be cumulative—for example, an officer may investigate too many child sexual abuse cases.) The psychological trauma can adversely affect an officer's mental attitude at both work and home.

As a professional criminal justice supervisor, you should be well-versed in the identification and understanding of this phenomenon. After all, it is one of your responsibilities to take care of your people. Most progressive agencies have an outlet to assist traumatized officers. It may be a department peer counseling group or a formal employee assistance program. Whatever resources your agency has, be familiar with them and refer your employees to these resources as needed. Do whatever you can to maintain the employee's confidentiality should they seek assistance. It can often be difficult for many employees to seek this help on their own, so do your part to facilitate this.

REVIEW QUESTIONS:

1. Why is preparation such a critical factor in handling critical incidents?

2. Why is it important for a criminal justice supervisor to respond to a critical incident?

3. What role does leadership play in a supervisor's response to a critical incident?

4. Why should a critical incident report be written as soon as possible after the conclusion of the incident?

5. What is a criminal justice supervisor's role regarding post-incident trauma?

CHAPTER 12

Supervisory Response to Critical Incidents—Part II

There are some critical incidents that are so frequent, so highly liable or just career threatening for all those involved, that we wanted to give you some specific insights and advice on these topics.

If your criminal justice agency has specific policies, procedures and guidelines on these topics, then be sure that you know and follow these policies and procedures. And, if any of the following types of incidents come to your attention, be sure that you, or another highly competent supervisor, responds and documents everything regarding the incident. That will help you to protect the personnel involved, your agency and the public that you serve.

Deadly force incidents

There may be no more critical incident that requires you, as a criminal justice supervisor, to exhibit your greatest leadership ability. Whether the use of deadly force was against a civilian or an officer, you must take command and do things right. Your employees and the public demand it, and both will hold you accountable for what you do and how well you do it.

Your first priority after arriving at the scene should be to treat the injured, or see that those who are treating the injured have the resources, manpower and support that is necessary. The dead will wait. Your primary responsibility is the treatment of the injured first. If officers and suspects are both injured, your obligation is to both! Professional triage priorities should govern your actions.

You also must remember that this is a crime scene. Regardless of who shot whom or any subsequent justifications by law, this is a homicide or serious assault crime scene and must be protected for the preservation of evidence. That may include restricting access or cordoning off the area, consistent with getting help to the injured. This can be challenging, especially if there are still suspects to be apprehended in the area. Keep officer and civilian safety in mind as well.

You must also make the appropriate notifications to your bosses. But, even after you notify your supervisor, you are still in charge of, and responsible for, the scene until you are relieved by a superior. We suggest proceeding with the scene and the investigation as if you will never be relieved and must conduct the entire investigation to its conclusion.

Then, there is the media to deal with. Critical incidents will nearly always draw them to your scene. When they arrive, you must know your agency's policies and procedures in dealing with them. Do they get special access to the crime scene? How far away should they be? Who should talk to them? Answer all of these questions in your own mind before the incident ever occurs, then implement your policies confidently, no matter who challenges them.

Keep in mind that there will be a thorough investigation, or sometimes multiple investigations, conducted in any use of force situation. They may be done by a special shooting team, internal affairs, the F.B.I., the State Police, the district attorney may call for a special investigation, or maybe it will just be your investigation. It all depends on your agency and the circumstances. Just proceed with your duties and let the scene, the evidence, and witness statements take you wherever they go. Whether the use of force was legally justified or not will be up to a grand jury or the district attorney to decide. Keep in mind that your job is to treat the injured, safeguard the scene and collect the evidence and statements to the best of your ability.

You can also help your people by having a good understanding of post-incident trauma. Your people go through a lot in any use of force incident. Your actions at the scene, and your follow-up actions later, can have a big influence on how your people handle the stress of such a traumatic event. Try to take a course in post-incident trauma and learn what you can do to prevent it or reduce its effects. Such a training course is beyond the scope of this book, but do yourself, and your people, a favor by finding and signing up for such a course before a critical deadly physical force incident occurs in your unit.

Injuries to people in custody

Just short of a deadly force incident is the critical incident where an individual is injured being taken into custody, prior to being taken into custody or while in custody. Such incidents are fairly common in many segments of the criminal justice system. All of these injuries need to be taken seriously by a criminal justice supervisor and they need to be thoroughly investigated and documented. To do so can protect your officers from wrongful allegations, as well as protecting the rights of citizens against abuse.

The same rules apply as in most other critical incident situations, Treat the injured first, Get photographs of the injuries and secure other physical evidence. Make appropriate supervisory notifications and take statements from all involved. Let your people know why you are conducting such a thorough investigation and assure them that it is being done to protect everyone involved. Once they understand what you are doing and why, they are likely to help you all they can.

Role of the supervisor in vehicle pursuits

First, you must know your agency's pursuit policy cold. And, prior to any pursuit you must be sure that your people know what your agency's pursuit policy is. It's your job to be sure they know.

When a pursuit begins, you must be sure that the dispatcher notifies you. Then you must monitor the pursuit to be sure that it is being conducted consistent with your agency's policies and the safety of your officers and public.

As a supervisor who is not at the scene, your role may be as simple as asking on the radio: "Is it correct that you are pursuing for speeding only?" Such a statement will remind the adrenaline-charged officer that speeding is not an offense for which your policies allow pursuit. It can also serve to put the pursuit, and its inherent dangers, in perspective for the officer on the street.

Other considerations you must evaluate as you monitor the

pursuit may include the number of vehicles involved, the jurisdictions involved, the necessity of the pursuit, traffic conditions, and a host of other variables and options to safely ending the pursuit.

And, finally, you must control the end of a pursuit when adrenaline-charged officers will directly confront the subjects of the pursuit, up close and personal. Even though you can't be there, the attitude and guidelines you and your agency have set down must be followed by your on-scene personnel. Your leadership of having instilled the concept of "always do the right thing" can prevent any excessive force in such situations.

Forcible stopping of vehicles

A request for permission to ram a vehicle should never be heard over a radio. Yet, consistent with your agency's policies and procedures, such "legal intervention" as it is known, may or may not be appropriate in a given situation. Many departments prohibit it completely, while others allow legal intervention under limited circumstances.

The reason that a request for permission to ram should never be heard over the radio is because your people already know your agency's policies on legal intervention, and the factors and consequences of their actions in such cases. That doesn't happen accidentally. You, as a team supervisor, must have already prepared them for this possible eventuality.

The same concept holds true for spinning out cars, the use of spike strips, moving roadblocks, stationary roadblocks, etc. Before you or your people attempt the use of any of these tactics, be sure that everyone knows the policies and procedures of the department, and the consequences of their use to affect the forcible stopping of a motor vehicle. Preparedness, policy, safety, and judgment are the keys to your successful leadership in these cases.

Civil rights incidents

Responsible people can disagree. And, the voices of both sides are protected under the United States Constitution. Their rights include the right of peaceful assembly and the right of freedom of speech.

But, the rights of one person can infringe on the rights of another person.

The laws and their interpretation by the courts tend to strike a balance between competing interests. But, it is up to the criminal justice professional to know and uphold the rulings of the courts. So, whether the conflict involves labor strikes, pro vs. anti-abortion advocates, or NIMBY's (not-in-my-backyard) opponents to public or private projects, criminal justice professionals are charged with keeping them peaceful.

First, there is no right to civil disobedience—not in the Constitution, not in the Bill of Rights, not in the laws of the state or the municipality where the incident is occurring. All citizens must obey the law. However, criminal justice professionals, the police in particular, must use good judgment and discretion in enforcing the laws.

Officers must protect both sides during any confrontation or conflict, whether or not they agree with one side or the other. And, as a supervisor, you must ensure that your people remain neutral in any situation. You must remind them of their central role and their mission of maintaining order consistent with Constitutional safeguards.

And, that brings us to the most critical issue in civil rights and police/citizen confrontation. You must protect your people, particularly if a volatile situation starts to erupt. As a police commander, on the scene at a critical incident, you have several options available to you. You may "hold the line," until additional help arrives, you may "fall back" until help arrives, or you may "move forward" to quell a potentially riotous or dangerous situation before it gets out of hand.

The decision will be yours often without direction or counsel. Your decision will be critical, both for the safety of your people and to the maintenance of public safety. You must carefully, within moments, accurately assess the situation, make your decision and implement it.

If, as a commander, you choose to commit your forces to a legitimate goal (i.e., dispersing a potentially violent crowd, breaking down illegal barriers, entering a building that protesters may be blocking, etc.), be sure that your people have a "reasonable expectation of winning." For example, if you decide to clear a street, be sure that you have adequate manpower and equipment to do so, and be sure the crowd is left an outlet so they are able to disperse. Otherwise, hold the line until you are confident that you have the people and equipment to do so.

Be there at the scene, and lead your people to do what is right to protect citizens, your people and citizens' rights.

Off-duty incidents

The public often holds its criminal justice personnel to a higher standard of conduct than the members of the general population. They may view police, parole, probation and correction officers as holders of their "public trust." However, the price of that trust is a higher standard of personal conduct.

So, what happens when an off-duty criminal justice professional is involved in any type of controversial incident like a late-night auto accident, or a confrontation in a bar, or even a neighborhood dispute? Well, most anything can happen, so when you get word of such an incident, you'd better respond and sort it out.

Off-duty incidents have often damaged an employee's credibility or sometimes even the credibility of the entire organization. Sort it out, document it, take statements and make appropriate supervisory notifications. These types of incidents can explode in the media or at a later time after the rumors have circulated. You had better do your job as a supervisor! Let the chips fall where they may. Your officers are not perfect, and if they step out of line, exceed or abuse their authority or even if they are just plain wrong, it was their off-duty conduct that put them there. You just do your job and document everything. That may exonerate them or condemn them, but you have done your job by objectively investigating and documenting the incident. Anything less than that could put your own career in jeopardy.

Celebrity incidents

Any criminal justice involvement with politicians, actors, rock stars or any other celebrity should come to your attention. And, you should respond to and sort it all out. Document it, write a report, etc., etc. All you need to do is watch a celebrity TV show or read a newspaper tabloid to know that incidents are exposed, hyped and examined, sometimes truthfully, but more often, not so truthfully.

Cover your people, yourself, and your agency by responding and documenting what you find. Make appropriate supervisory notifications so that no one in your chain of command is "blind-sided" by the media or media accounts. So, whether it is a county supervisor who is arrested for D.W.I., or a professional football player involved in a bar fight or a rock star arrested for drug possession, you must respond and handle it—professionally!

We have covered some of the more typical examples of critical incidents that you may encounter, but, of course, every job has its own peculiarity, and we cannot cover every type of incident in every one of your criminal justice agencies. But, we can give you some guidance on this topic. First, let your people know that you want to know about serious or unusual incidents. Make sure they know your agency's policy on when you need to be notified. And, even if your agency does not have a policy on "Supervisory Notification," you should write up a memo for your officers telling them exactly what you expect them to do and when you expect to be notified. That way, later on, there won't be any questions about your role in the incident. This is absolutely critical in small agencies that may lack supervisory coverage 24/7. Then, if they call you at midnight, it's probably important enough for you to respond. If it turns out to be nothing critical, you can always go back home and go back to bed. But, our experience has been that if it's important enough to call a supervisor, it's important enough to respond to and document.

Trust us. Critical incidents such as we have discussed here are career-making and career-breaking. When it all blows up, if you did your job, it is likely to "blow over" in short order. If you did not do your job, your officer is likely to say: "But I told the boss," and that loud noise you hear might be the sound of your criminal justice career imploding!

REVIEW QUESTIONS:

1. Why is a "use of deadly force scene" considered a crime scene?

2. Why should a criminal justice supervisor be well-versed on the subject of post-incident trauma?

3. Who is responsible for officers knowing the agency's pursuit policy?

4. Why is an officer's off-duty conduct of interest to a criminal justice agency?

5. What is likely to happen to your criminal justice career if you do not properly and effectively respond to and handle critical incidents as a supervisor?

CHAPTER 13

Media Relations

You have a problem, Sergeant!

A media photographer has shown up at the scene of a fatal car accident and begins snapping photographs for the local newspaper. One of your officers tells the photographer to stop taking photos, but he ignores your officer, flashes his media credentials and continues to walk towards the car wreck. Now your officer starts yelling at the photographer and tells him that if he takes any more photos that he will be placed under arrest, using force if necessary. Under physical threat, the photographer backs off. Several months later, the photographer files a federal civil rights lawsuit against your officer, you, and your agency, claiming that his First Amendment rights were violated because he was forced to stop taking photographs, that he was "deprived of property interest," and deprived of his "livelihood without due process of law," as guaranteed under the Fourteenth Amendment. The photographer also claims that you and the agency are guilty of negligent supervision and negligent retention. The newspaper's lawyers are filing paperwork and there are big stories about this case every day in the newspaper. Wow! You got a major incident on your hands. Did your officer do the right thing? Did you do the right thing as a supervisor? Could a major incident like this have been avoided?

(We don't make up stuff like this . . . see *Kinsey v. City of Opp (AL)*, et al., 50 F.Supp2d 1232 (1999)

Managing the media

All agencies in the criminal justice system are newsmakers. When a prisoner escapes from police custody, when a judge is attacked in a courtroom or a suspect is shot during a police chase, the media will be on the phone, at your door and in your face. As a criminal justice professional, you need to anticipate interaction with the media, and you need to be thoroughly prepared to deal and work with them, consistent with your agency's policies and procedures.

Most criminal justice agencies don't do enough to prepare people like you to deal with the media. And, this chapter will only provide a brief overview of media relations. So where does that leave you as an upwardly mobile criminal justice supervisor? That means it's up to you to start preparing yourself to handle media situations. First, get out your policy and procedure manual and learn whatever guidelines there are for you. How far should crime scene lines be away from the actual crime scene? Does the media get special access beyond what the general public gets? Who is authorized in your agency to speak to the media? What do you do if you're asked to be interviewed on camera? Answer these, and many more media relations questions from your policy manual. If your agency has a public information officer, get to know him or her. Ask questions—get guidance.

Managing media relations is the same as any other aspect of managing your career. You must get all of the education, training and experience that you can on the topic, and then apply it to the situation that you will face. So, if your agency does not provide a course on media relations, go take a media relations course from another agency. Contact a local college and take appropriate journalism courses. Go online and see what courses you can take to improve your understanding of, and your interaction with, the media.

Let's start here by defining the media, who they are and what do they want? They range from your local weekly newspaper to your local radio station and on to the reporter from your local, and sometimes nationally affiliated, TV station. And, don't forget the "stringers"—ordinary citizens who get paid by the media for a photograph or a video of a crime scene or other controversial scene where you might be. What they want is information. An event has occurred and they feel it is their duty to get that information and give it to the public. Nearly all of these people are college educated, and may have degrees in journalism. They vary widely in experience, but rest assured, that they will use all of their own education, training and experience to get what they want, and that is information—names, times, photographs and details.

And, whether it is the local weekly newspaper or the TV station getting a story for the 6 o'clock television news, they all have specific deadlines they must meet to file their stories. So time is of the essence as they gather information to put into their stories. If they don't get accurate and complete information from you or your agency, then they will get their information from some other sources. That 'other source' might be a pseudo-expert on the topic who knows little about the specifics of your incident, but can "wing it" for thirty seconds of criticism of you and your agency. They may also fill their print space or airtime with "man on the street" interviews of neighbors, witnesses or the general public. "Do you feel that the police use excessive force in too many of these types of incidents?" They will edit and air whatever they get from these interviews.

Add to this situation the general distrust that some of the media may have for members of the criminal justice community, and vice versa. When one consultant brought members of the media into the same classroom as members of various police agencies, he asked them to list three adjectives that described the other group. Law enforcement described the media as "demanding," "unethical," "uncaring," "biased," "arrogant," and "negative." The media participants described the police as "evasive," "uncooperative," "not trustable," "self-important," "indifferent," and "withholding." There were some positive comments as well, but you get the picture.

As with other aspects of your job, media relations presents a challenge for you as a criminal justice professional. You can ignore it and refuse to deal with the media. In that case, your people and your agency will be at the mercy of every reporter that has a need for information and coverage. OR, you can professionally manage your media relations so that you can adequately protect victims, witnesses, cases, your people and your agency. If you want to set yourself apart from your competition for promotion, learn to effectively deal with the media.

In addition to a thorough knowledge of your agency's policies and procedures regarding media relations, you should have a thorough understanding of how to effectively handle the media so that they can effectively do their jobs, while you and your people can effectively do their jobs. We strongly recommend that you get adequate training in the area of media relations. The higher you go in your agency, the more important this area of managing your career will become. That way, you will know what to do when you arrive at work one morning and your secretary says: "Chief, a couple of reporters from '60 Minutes' are waiting for you."

Be prepared!

1. Be "camera smart"—Cameras are everywhere . . . even if you can't see them. Even if you can see them, by then it might be too late! Not all cameras are held by the press. It used to be in the "old days" when the big spotlight of the camera came on, it was time to behave. No more! Many cameras are compact, low-light, and used by civilians, often from long distances. (Remember the Rodney King videotape?) Many citizens are waiting for you or one of your officers to say something or do something so they can make money from the media who will buy the tape from them. Nowadays cameras are extremely small and do not need floodlights at night. Reporters and civilians have rights and they will always misinterpret what is on the film. This should not influence you in how you handle a situation, but you may have to justify what you did or said if it gets in the news.

2. Notify your boss if something negative has been done or said—The media will air it anyway, but warning your boss will allow them time to do "damage control." Your administration should address the matter first by taking the offense and explaining the police-side of the matter first, before the media gets a chance to make you look bad. Your actions will still be questioned by the media, but your agency can tell their side of the story.

3. *Never* say: "No comment"—If you do, you are almost guaranteed to look guilty. This is the same as someone taking the "Fifth Amendment" in court. Learn to be creative and positive. Don't give away any information, but

learn to respond like a politician. Say something without really saying something.

4. Always explain "why"—Explain why you can't give out information. There is a big difference between a gruff "No comment," and a polite "I can't offer a detailed response to any of your questions at this time. The Public Information Officer (or Chief . . . or somebody) will provide you with details as soon as possible." Now, the media doesn't get what they want, but you also don't sound like you're hiding something. You also look like a "good guy" by at least pretending to cooperate.

There is much more to effectively dealing with the media, but we have limited space here. We strongly recommend that you pursue additional training in media relations from other sources. Trust us once again; it will be good for your career to be well trained in this area.

REVIEW QUESTIONS:

1. What are five ways that a criminal justice professional can "manage" the media?

2. How can you be prepared for the media when you are involved in a critical incident?

3. Who should be notified if the media catches something they can interpret as "negative" on video or audio?

4. Why is "No comment" an unacceptable comment to the media?

5. Why is knowledge and training in media relations a good idea for your career development?

CHAPTER 14

Communications

Communication comes in a variety of forms. In early times, commanders in battle would use flags on hilltops to communicate with their troops on the field of battle. Certain flags had certain meanings, whether to charge, commit a cavalry, or to retreat. During the Civil War, commanders used young boys to carry communiques and orders between their field units using shallow communication trenches. The boys, some as young as twelve years old, were placed in serious danger, but generally got those communiques through to the field commanders, and back. They were a key component in the communication process, even though most of them could not read or write.

For today's modern criminal justice leaders the same basic rules of the Civil War are still applicable. There is a communication "process" today that can involve several components. First, the communications or order must be effectively thought out. Then it must be "given out" in some form, generally oral or written. It must have an effective delivery system, analogous to the flags or couriers of old. Then, it must be understandable, effectively interpreted and then executed by the recipients.

There are possible pitfalls at every level of the communication process. The original plan could be flawed, or the words used in issuing a command or directive can be unclear to the recipient. The delivery method could be interrupted and the message or order could be delayed, or never received. Even if it arrives intact, the recipient could misinterpret the order, or put their own "spin" on it so that the original intent is stymied or lost. In short, communication is an inexact science. Given that, let's try to learn how to communicate as effectively as possible, given the pitfalls and problems of the process. Your effectiveness as a criminal justice professional must rely on your being an effective communicator, both in operational and administrative matters.

General communication skills

There are three basic communication skills to master.

1. The first is speaking. In order to be a successful leader you must master this skill to some degree. First, your basic speech must be understood by others. Therefore, you must learn to speak without a heavy geographic or ethnic accent. If people can't understand your words, they can't understand your orders.

   You must also be capable of speaking in public. To some people their fear of speaking in public paralyzes their otherwise capable performance. If you think you might have trouble in this area, take a public speaking course or courses at a local college. It will provide you with the basic skills and will help to build the confidence you need to speak in public. And, if you will be speaking in public, prepare-prepare-prepare, by doing your homework on facts and figures. And, of course, practice before you go.

2. The second basic communication skill is the ability to write effectively. You don't need to be able to write like Hemingway, but you do need to be able to write an effective memo, directive or order. Your writing should be direct, to the point, and as sensible as you can make it so it is easily understood by the recipient. And, once it is on paper, you can't take it back. It might as well be embedded in stone. So, be sure of what you want to say, and be sure it cannot be misinterpreted, before it goes to print.

   Does grammar count? You bet it does. Your writing is a reflection of your personality and your personal skills. The quality of your written order communicates a great deal about who you are and how competent you are. Check your work for proper grammar and spelling before it goes out in written form.

3. The ability to listen is also a valuable communication skill for every commander. You need to listen to your bosses, your peers and your subordinates. They all have valuable information to share with you to help you identify problems, evaluate your options and generate solutions and effective decisions.

Non-verbal communication

Above and beyond the "words" of written or oral communication are the observable actions involved in effective communication. The words can often be "spoken," but other actions belie their meaning. Just as when you were interviewing suspects, as a supervisor or commander you can use the same skills when dealing with personnel matters.

Posture reveals attitude. Eye contact can convey honesty, reveal deception or expose an insecurity. Invading someone's "personal space" can help reveal a person's level of security, or evoke an emotional response. And, of course, body movements such as restlessness, unusual responses and nervous tics can be very revealing. These responses may be physical, but they still fall under the general category of communication, and a commander needs to be able to recognize and master them.

Communications in organizations

Commanders of all ranks need to understand how communications work in their organizations. First, there is downward communication. This comes from the top commanders, down to the rank and file through a process generally known as the chain of command. The Chief or department head, usually with input from advisors, sends out a directive or memo that all ranks are to receive and follow.

Then, there can also be upward communication. This can be as simple as talking to your boss at any level in the organization. You should be able to accept any communication from anyone below your rank in the organization with an eye towards accepting their input. How much of it you send up to your boss, or bosses, is a matter of professional judgment on your part.

Informal communications

Much of what we have just described is "formal" communication (memos, interviews, etc). Generally, this is "on the record" and can be quoted, documented or formalized in some other way. Yet, much of the communications in a criminal justice organization falls into the "informal" category. This can take the form of casual conversation over a cup of coffee or an "off the record" kind of verbal conversation with a boss or subordinate. Although much information can be conveyed this way for the betterment of the organization during these "informal" contacts, a word of caution is given here.

Beware when someone wants to talk to you in strict confidence. Be aware, and make them aware, that whatever is revealed will be in confidence with certain limitations. You cannot, as a commander, receive certain information without later acting on it. This can include evidence of criminal activity, sexual harassment, discrimination issues, etc. In these cases you must act on, or reveal the information or evidence, in order to fulfill your supervisory obligations or face problems yourself when it finally comes out that your employee says, "I told my supervisor about this." Then there is no hiding your head in the sand. You had better have done the right thing.

Informal communications can be a valuable tool for the astute criminal justice manager who uses it wisely. But, handle "informal" communications very carefully to avoid the pitfalls.

Barriers to effective communication

There are several barriers to effective communications that criminal justice supervisors and managers must overcome. We have listed some of them.

Physical barriers: In large organizations, physical distance can be a problem. Remote stations or sectors can increase communication problems.

Psychological barriers: Sometimes subordinates just don't want to hear it, so they don't. Supervisors must overcome this "attitude" problem.

Ambiguous words: There are so many "relative" terms in the English language. Some examples are "timely," "forthwith," "reasonable," "unreasonable," "sooner," "later," "appropriate," "inappropriate," . . . You get the picture. Be concise and to the point.

Selective listening: Just as your people sometimes hear only what they want to hear, you may do the same.

Filtering: This is the process where your people "filter" what they say to you. They may only give you the good news and not tell you any bad news. And, unless you work at it, you may not have a clue until the bad news blows up and you have a serious problem because "you should have known."

Distortion: If you have ever done an exercise consisting of several people consecutively relaying a verbal message to one another you know how frustrating person-to-person communication can be. Somehow, "The Chief wants all members to be professional and accountable for their actions," can quickly turn into: "Internal affairs is investigating every citizen contact." Be aware and investigate and control all rumors.

Confusion: Ambiguous words and phrases can lead to confusion. Do your best to write clear, concise and understandable orders and directives. Follow up on all orders to be sure there is no confusion.

Assumption: Assumptions are always dangerous. Ask questions, get clarifications, and don't act on assumptions.

Timing: Departmental, national and local events can affect the timing of effective communications of any criminal justice organization. And, any critical local incident can affect the meaning of any directive or order.

As an example, after a special interest group has recently been very vocal about police tactics in general, it is not a great time to issue an order dramatically changing certain police procedures or tactics. The rank and file may view that move as capitulation to a special interest group's words, even though the two events are unrelated. Perception can become reality.

If you have taken nothing else from this chapter, take away the fact that total communication—written, oral or non-verbal, is imprecise. What you say and do can be interrupted in various ways by your people and can adversely affect the mission involved. Communicate as effectively and precisely as you can. You will make a few errors along the way, but if you work at it, you will become an effective communicator. And the better you can communicate, both orally and through the written word, the higher you will go in your organization.

REVIEW QUESTIONS:

1. Why is communication such an inexact science?

2. What are the three basic communication skills a commander should master?

3. What role can non-verbal communications play in the communications process?

4. What should you do if someone wants to talk to you in strict confidence?

5. Name three barriers to effective communication?

CHAPTER 15

Documentation

"If it isn't on paper, it didn't happen," is a phrase that you will want to remember throughout your career. For every unusual incident you or your people get involved in, for every personnel action you take or don't take, there needs to be some form of permanent or semi-permanent documentation. You never know what lies ahead of you in your role as a supervisor. For example, you may need evidence of what originally occurred at an incident when you are about to testify about it at a future criminal or civil trial, unemployment, workmen's compensation or disciplinary hearing. Neither you, nor others, will ever recollect the facts or circumstances as accurately as if you had documented them at the time of the incident, or shortly thereafter.

So, resign yourself right now to the concept that the paperwork necessary to document incidents, etc. is just a natural part of being a criminal justice supervisor. If you learn to document things well, then you resolve conflicts and prove that you and your people did what was right at the time and under the circumstances, because you documented it and made a permanent or semi-permanent record that you can now produce.

Types of documentation

Just like a police officer's investigation of a crime, when you arrive on the scene of an incident, you must identify the witnesses, secure evidence and take notes, that may later be turned into a formal report, or not, depending on what the incident is and how seriously the incident needs to be fully documented.

As an example: Suppose that you are a police supervisor and one of your police officers is involved in a property damage accident, with a police car striking a civilian's auto at an intersection. You are called to the scene. You take notes and statements from the civilian driver, any witnesses, and maybe, depending on your policies and procedures, from your employee. It takes a while to do all this and much of your time will be spent doing the formal accident report, attaching the statements and verifying all of the circumstances, all for a simple property damage accident. You file this routine report with your department. Three months later, your department lawyer advises you that your officer and department are being sued civilly for your officer causing the accident in which the civilian driver and several passengers were severely injured. You are even named in the lawsuit for "failure to actively supervise" your officer and they allude to negligence on your part. The plaintiffs want big bucks!

Wait a minute—you were there . . . there were no injuries, and your officer was not at fault. Sounds like a totally different accident. But, you are not terribly concerned because you had documented everything and took written statements from everybody at the time of the accident. In short, you did your job and now your report and statements will save your officer, you, and the department. The bogus plaintiff's claim is likely to be thrown out once their attorney or the judge find out about the timely reports you filed on the incident.

This same type of scenario can be played out in use of force incidents, injuries to prisoners, high-speed chases and personnel matters. In fact, if you as a supervisor are called to the scene, the situation probably warrants some type of documentation, formal or informal. Remember, if it isn't on paper, it didn't happen—at least, not the way it really happened.

On-scene issues

In any incident, you will want to document the circumstances of the incident, and who was there, including personnel higher in rank than you. Take statements from all witnesses, at the time, so they can't change their stories later. Take good notes in a professional-looking notebook or daybook that you use solely for business.

Remember, your notes may be subpoenaed or entered into evidence at a later date. So, take good notes and keep your grocery list in another booklet.

Don't forget to take photos, whenever appropriate, of injuries, damage—or the absence of injury or damage. One officer was saved from an unjust prisoner brutality case because of a routine mugshot that was taken after the alleged brutality occurred. Turns out the young man's father beat him up after he got home because he had gotten arrested. They then conspired to claim the arresting officer had caused the facial injuries. Their attorney filed a brutality lawsuit based on their word. The lawsuit was ultimately thrown out and the father and son arrested for filing a false report, all because of one routine photo. That's how important documentation can be.

Report writing

You may, depending on the circumstance, turn your notes into a formal report of some type, depending on the severity of the incident and the policies and procedures of your department. A good practical gauge is that even if you remotely think you should write a report on the incident—do it. It will save you problems later if you just go ahead and write the report. And, of course, the standard report writing rules apply:

> Who?
> What?
> Where?
> When?
> Why?
> How?
> Complete, neat and timely.

Writing a good report will set you apart from supervisors who are less conscientious or who don't get the "big picture" of their role as a criminal justice supervisor. Your superior officers will notice that difference and that will bode well for your future career in your agency.

Other types of documentation

Many supervisors carry a simple "diary" which is a bound book with one page for each day of the year. This diary is used for documenting supervisory responses and actions on each day. They record June 25th for example, with entries such as:

> Working "C" shift.
> At roll call, presented a five-minute program on the new changes in department pursuit policy.
>
> At 9 pm found Officer Fitzgerald out of her assigned sector. Counseled verbally. No Report.
>
> 11:15 pm responded to robbery in progress call. Perp apprehended by patrol prior to my arrival. No supervisory action taken.

These simple entries "document" what you did. They are a permanent record of your responses, training and actions. It is far short of a report, but certainly could save you or others in a pinch, because it is documentation that you were there.

Other forms of documentation can include memos either written to you, or by you, documenting some fact or circumstances. The memo, dated and written at or around the time of an incident, tends to serve as documentation. An example might be an unusually irate motorist one of your police officers gave a ticket to. There is no allegation of officer misconduct by the motorist, but the officer "just wanted you to know" that the motorist was irate and threatened the officer that he would "have your job!" Document it with a dated memo of the circumstances as related to you by your officer, just in case it blows up a week from now with an inquiry from the mayor's office.

Still other forms of documentation you will want to spend time putting together include those found in your formal personnel evaluation system. Some limitations may be placed on your documentation efforts by departmental policies or by formal labor agreements. But, in general, your documentation should include the notes you make on the accomplishments and counseling of your employees. Often, these are kept in a "rating" file and can include such things as commendations, copies of outstanding or poor reports, as well as minor infractions of rules and regulations such as late or incomplete reports, counseling notes or memos, etc. You will generally use the contents of the rating file to put together and document a formal evaluation for each of your employees once or twice a year.

Training records

Any and all training that you or your people receive, from any source, should be documented. In many organizations, the training section or academy will keep such records, but that may not be enough. They may not include items like the fifteen minutes of training on sexual harassment prevention you did at the beginning of your shift last month. Every training session should be documented as to who was there, who gave the session and the length and subject matter. Such information should be included in every attending employee's personnel record. Particular attention should be paid by you, as a supervisor, in the high liability areas such as pursuit policies, sexual harassment prevention, discrimination issues and use of force issues. Be sure your people have adequate training in these areas and be sure that such training is documented. After the lawsuits are filed is no time to try to blame the training section for not keeping good records. You, as a criminal justice supervisor, are responsible for the training of your personnel. Do it, and document it!

And, pay particular attention to your own training records. Be sure that you can produce, on a moment's notice, a complete record of your own training. That would include keeping an up-to-date "running resume" as well as being able to produce appropriate diplomas and certificates of completion for all of your past training. Not only may that come in handy before a promotional board, but it will be great information to have in case a plaintiff's or defense attorney asks you the question, "What, if any, training have you had to be a criminal justice supervisor?"

All of the forms of documentation we have discussed, when completed properly, can help to protect you, your people and the department by providing a semi-permanent or permanent record of events, at or near, the time they occurred. Documentation is a critical part of a criminal justice supervisor's job description. We know you didn't become a criminal justice professional just to do paperwork, but you must accept it as a part of your job. Because remember: "If it isn't on paper, it didn't happen."

REVIEW QUESTIONS:

1. Why is documentation a critical part of a police supervisor's job?

2. What are the five W's of report writing?

3. What is the purpose of keeping a Diary?

4. Who does adequate documentation of incidents protect?

5. What is the purpose of a "rating file?"

CHAPTER 16

Motivation and Morale

The first line supervisor is the most important factor and influence on the performance of people under his/her command. Every supervisor, at every level of the organization, must learn to recognize what motivates each individual member of their unit. Everyone is different and has different needs, desires and goals. Recognizing and acting upon those differences is how a supervisor motivates the individuals in the unit, for the benefit of the unit's mission and goals.

The importance of recognizing what motivates the people under your command cannot be overestimated. Proper motivation leads to good morale in a unit, and good morale leads to the success of the unit. Subordinates of excellent supervisors have excellent morale. Subordinates of poor supervisors have poor morale.

So, if the morale in your unit seems to be low, you are the most likely cause and it's time to make a positive change.

Positive incentives that motivate

Let's start out by talking about the positive incentives for your people to do a good job in their everyday activities. You actually control many of these "positive buttons." Employees can be motivated by:

1. Receiving recognition for their good work.
2. Being praised for their good work and efforts.
3. Having the opportunity for personal development.
4. Having an interesting and challenging job.
5. Being treated fairly.

Supervisors can also negatively influence their people through the use of negative incentives. These negative tools are employed by some supervisors, but their effects on motivation are often short-lived, and they generally adversely affect morale. They include:

1. Fear
2. Coercion
3. Intimidation
4. Punishment
5. Unfairness

The most effective supervisor is the one who creates the proper climate for his/her people to enjoy their jobs and flourish in their personal accomplishments. That supervisor will treat everyone fairly. Notice we didn't say "equally" because everyone is different. All people in the workplace may have equal rights under the law, but they are not equal in their needs, desires and goals. And, each individual brings to the workplace individual strengths and weaknesses. A good supervisor treats everyone fairly and recognizes and respects the differences between individual employees.

Good supervisors expect, and generally have the right to demand good work from all of the employees under his/her command. That said, "good work" is a relative term. What is good work from one person with excellent skills, abilities and training, may be excellent performance from someone with lesser skills, abilities and training. Therefore, it is necessary to treat people and their performances individually, factoring in their personal strengths and weaknesses.

The effective criminal justice supervisor also goes to whatever lengths are necessary to protect his/her people from the "predators" in, and around, an organization who can disrupt order and morale in a unit. Those predators can include other commanders and administrators who place unrealistic burdens on your people. They can also include competing groups from within your organization or external special interest groups who will badmouth your people for their own gain. You must maintain a constant vigil in order to protect your people if you are to maintain their support and keep up their morale.

Maslow's Hierarchy of Needs

In an effort to understand exactly what motivates human beings in the workplace, one researcher studied individuals and groups and developed the following theory of human motivation. Known as Maslow's Hierarchy of Needs, the needs are listed in a pyramid style, with the most basic needs being on the bottom of the pyramid, and the other needs listed on the higher levels of the pyramid. As each level of need is satisfied, the motivation need of that individual moves to the next higher level on the pyramid. Here, listed from lowest to highest on that pyramid are Maslow's findings:

1. First, workers have the most basic of human needs. Known as physiological needs, they include the basics of life including air, food, shelter, and sex. Without these needs fulfilled, people are not happy and the possibilities for good performance in the workplace are slim. Most everyone employed in criminal justice has these needs met.

2. The next need in Maslow's hierarchy is the need for safety and security. People want safe working conditions and benefits for the welfare of themselves and their families. These include general salary increases and job security. The latter benefits are usually provided in most public service jobs, but certainly the first line supervisor can influence the safety and security aspect of an officer's inherently dangerous job, by ensuring against "needless" risks brought on by poor leadership or poor tactics.

Also, in trying to satisfy this level, some supervisors make the mistake of using the wrong method to motivate. For example, you may not be motivating an employee when you offer them a chance to work overtime. You might think you are helping them because "I thought he could use a little more money," but in reality, the employee might be overworked as it is and would really like a day's comp. time to spend with his family.

3. The next need on Maslow's hierarchy of needs include the social needs of individuals in the workplace. Employees in all industries want professional friendships with

their co-workers. They also want an overall compatible work group, free of unnecessary conflict. Also under this category of need is that employees want a good quality of supervisor; not too much, not too little, and always professional. That would be your job.

Sometimes some very good candidates for promotion choose not to take the test, and this can be frustrating for administrators who want the best candidates promoted. But, perhaps this employee is 'satisfied' on this level of needs. They like the group they are working with, they like the shift they are on, they like the boss they currently have. They choose not to take the promotional test for fear of being promoted to a different shift, or in some larger criminal justice agencies (state and federal in particular), a promotion often means moving, and this can be viewed as a reason **not** to get promoted.

4. Moving higher on the list of workplace needs, we move to the category of ego, status, and self-esteem. This includes the fact that people want a degree of responsibility, and that work itself can be rewarding. They also want good peer/supervisor relations, a good and prestigious job and merit pay increases based on their exceptional performance.

5. At the top of Maslow's pyramid is the self-actualization phase. Employees have achieved all of the foregoing needs and now want the feeling of achievement in their work, advancement in the organization, a challenging job and the freedom to be able to create innovative solutions they can apply to the job and its problems.

Good bosses realize that they have some very talented and creative people on their shift. And, good bosses allow these employees to take responsibility. Good bosses value the input of these creative employees and give them as many opportunities as possible. We are all human enough to have a need to be appreciated and valued, whether it is in our personal relationships or in the workplace.

Understanding Maslow's Hierarchy of Needs is a step toward understanding your people and how they will progress up the pyramid of needs and motivation. It is up to you to determine where everyone in your unit is in the chain so you can anticipate and motivate them as they progress ever higher in the hierarchy. It can be a challenging task. The best supervisors continually work at understanding and motivating each individual under their command. As a result, they achieve success and high morale for both the individuals in their unit, as well as a high level of morale for the entire unit.

Herzberg's Two-Factor Theory

Paralleling Maslow's work is Herzberg who came to similar conclusions, but divided the "needs" into two categories that he labeled "dissatisfiers" and "satisfiers."

Essentially, a "dissatisfier" is something that can make an employee unhappy, and therefore contribute to poor morale. A "satisfier" is essentially something that makes the worker happy and therefore contributes to a high morale and good performance. If the dissatisfiers are not adequate in the view of the employee, then the employees will be "dissatisfied" and therefore unhappy. But, once the dissatisfiers are quenched, employees can move on to the "satisfiers" and a higher level of morale.

Potential dissatisfiers can include:

1. Lack of job security
2. Inadequate salary
3. Poor working conditions
4. Lack of status
5. Poor organizational policies
6. Poor quality of the supervisor
7. Inadequate fringe benefits

From this list, there are some things you, as a supervisor, can directly control and some that you cannot directly control. You can certainly control #6 by being the best supervisor you can be and properly motivating your people. And, you may have direct or indirect control over many organizational policies and procedures. And even people in very poor working conditions can have high morale if they enjoy coming to work and working with, and for, good people. That would be you.

Satisfiers include:

1. Achievement
2. Recognition
3. Work itself
4. Responsibility
5. Advancement
6. Personal growth and development

On the list of "satisfiers" you can exert even more direct influence as a supervisor. You can recognize your employees' achievements, give them responsible assignments and help them grow and advance within the organization. Help them to identify and reach their individual goals and the morale of your unit will be good. (Sounds a lot like Theory Y or Maslow's Hierarchy of Needs, and some of the best from those other theories that you just read about. All of this stuff comes together like a jigsaw puzzle, once you know where the pieces are that you are looking for.)

Other theories on motivation and morale have been developed, but Maslow's and Herzberg's should provide you with good basic information and guidance to see what really motivates each individual in your unit. Ignore these findings at your own, and your unit's, peril. Remember, the subordinates of excellent supervisors have excellent morale. But, the subordinates of poor supervisors have poor morale.

How's the morale in your unit?

REVIEW QUESTIONS:

1. Why do subordinates of excellent supervisors have excellent morale? Why do subordinate of poor supervisors have poor morale?

2. Name three positive incentives that motivate.

3. Name three negative incentives.

4. How do Maslow's physiological and safety and security needs compare with Herzberg's potential dissatisfiers list?

CHAPTER 17

Personnel Problems

The success of the criminal justice system, and your success as a supervisor or manager, depends on good people. Every successful administrator or supervisor knows that having the right people in the right place at the right time is the key to any successful operation. In addition, public confidence in the criminal justice system depends on the day-to-day honesty and integrity of each person in the system. It is clear that "people" are the key to success at all levels in the criminal justice system.

Enlightened criminal justice administrators know the value of their employees. They direct their recruiters, human resource people and/or personnel officers to seek out, recruit, and hire, the very best applicants to fill vacancies in the organization. Once identified, these applicants are screened for physical and mental attributes that are necessary for success in the criminal justice field. In progressive organizations, extensive background investigations are conducted to ensure the honesty and integrity of each candidate. Once hired, the new employee is trained, sometimes in an academy setting, and/or learns the basics of his/her new position through an appropriate orientation program, on-the-job training, a mentoring program or other means.

With all that time, effort and money spent, you would think that the newest addition to your unit would be a model employee and a joy for any supervisor to have on their team. In a perfect world, that would be true. Of course, in a perfect world, we wouldn't need a criminal justice system!

Welcome to the real world where all is not perfect. Despite the best efforts to recruit the best people, pay and benefits in many jobs in the criminal justice system may not be competitive with other jobs. Or, the pay and benefits in your criminal justice agency is less than a nearby criminal justice agency and your better young employees tend to leave your agency for that higher-paying agency. Many good candidates don't want to deal with the stresses and dangers associated with many jobs in our field. At every level of the hiring process, there can be flaws in the system, errors in judgment or monetary shortfalls. The bottom line is that you, as a supervisor, will get the best new employee that your organization can give you, given all the constraints of their resources. And, in most cases, they will be better-than-average who will work hard and enhance the image of your organization.

But, occasionally, the system fails. What should have been an excellent employee fails to meet expectations. Allegations of abuse of power, or alcohol use, or drug abuse, or other negatives cloud the image of your organization or your unit. Or worse, your employee is the subject of the lead story on the 6 o'clock news. Of course, it may not necessarily be the new employee who has problems. It could be the 15-year veteran with an excellent record. Where did it all go wrong? More importantly, were you a part of it going all wrong? Did you do your job as a supervisor to prevent, or at least identify, potential problems?

First, let's put things in perspective. The reason why a story of a corrupt, inept or abusive criminal justice employee makes the 6 o'clock news is because it is unusual. In general, criminal justice personnel go about their business in a professional manner with few problems. But, as one criminal justice administrator stated: "The problem is that we have to recruit our new employees from the human race." Thus, with all the frailties, weaknesses and temptations that humans have, anything can happen. The important thing is that you are prepared to deal with it when it does happen.

When a class of criminal justice supervisors was asked about what they considered to be serious criminal justice personnel problems, they cited the following problems on their list:

1. burnout
2. alcohol abuse
3. drug use
4. family and marital problems

5. mental health problems
6. sick leave abuse
7. corruption
8. excessive force
9. inexperienced employees
10. insubordination

As a supervisor, it is your responsibility to identify the early stages of any of these problems. Then, it may be your responsibility to take some action before it reaches the 6 o'clock news. But, when do you step in and what can you do about any of these problems or others that might develop with your employees?

First and foremost, be prepared for these kinds of problems, whatever they might be. In some cases, you will be given training on how to recognize alcohol or drug abuse. Additional workshops may focus on problems such as burnout or other personnel problems. Be sure to attend such workshops. In the absence of such training, read up on the topics so you are prepared if these problems come up in your unit.

As a part of your preparation, you should read your policy and procedure manual in detail. You should know when you have the authority to relieve a person from duty, and the proper procedure to follow before and after you do so. Know what tests you can give or not give. In short, know your authority and that of others in your organization. In some cases, you may have to go to the personnel manuals of your city, county or state to find out what your authority is in such matters. Union contracts and other collective bargaining agreements can limit your options. In some cases, you may have different options for sworn or civilian employees in your unit. Learn them all and apply them appropriately. In short, prepare . . . prepare . . . prepare.

Armed with all that knowledge, you will be able to intervene and take the proper action at the appropriate time. What is the appropriate time? It will vary with the circumstances, but a couple of general guidelines would be when it substantially adversely affects the employee's job performance or when it impacts the honesty and integrity of themselves, your unit or your agency.

A word of caution is appropriate here. Unless you are alone and you must clearly act immediately to prevent harm, try to reach out to your boss or other appropriate management personnel in your agency. It is always better to approach serious personnel problems with a team-effort in place whenever possible.

So once you take action, do you just throw the employee out of your agency and send them to the unemployment line? Generally not. It can cost tens of thousands of dollars to recruit, screen and train a new employee. Experienced employees are very valuable to any organization.

Recognizing this, many organizations have employee assistance programs (EAP) where employees can receive help in many areas, such as credit counseling, stress, burnout, depression, alcohol and drug rehabilitation programs, etc. Employees can often access these programs anonymously. You may want to quietly and discretely make an employee aware of such programs at the early stages of a problem, thereby giving the employee some say in their future. Whatever action you choose, in any personnel problem situation, be sure that you are on solid legal, departmental and factual grounds. Be sure that you follow your organization's policies and procedures properly. And, try to get other members of your management team involved. Take any actions as discretely as possible and be sure to document all of your actions over time. Be prepared to stand by your decisions in any future hearings or lawsuits. And, be a professional all through the process.

It's not a matter of "if " you will encounter employee problems during your career, it is a matter of when and how often. How well you are prepared for them is entirely up to you. As one career criminal justice professional stated: "The technical problems are easy to handle, it's the people problems that are the hard ones to solve." You will find that statement to be true in your own career as well. Prepare . . . prepare . . . prepare for that fact, if you want to have a successful career as a criminal justice professional.

REVIEW QUESTIONS

1. Name three steps of the recruitment and hiring process that can present problems in hiring the best possible people?

2. Why can personnel problems in the criminal justice system be such a news story on the 6 o'clock news?

3. List five serious personnel problems you may be forced to confront during your career.

4. What written resources should you consult for your authority to handle specific personnel problems?

5. What benefits are there to assembling a "management team" to help address a personnel problem?

CHAPTER 18

Discrimination

The term "discrimination" means to "make a distinction or judgment" and "to treat favorably or unfavorably in comparison with others." And, if you think about it, you will make such judgments every day of your criminal justice career. The only question is whether or not your "discrimination" is legal or illegal under existing laws.

In your day-to-day supervisory responsibilities, you will make perfectly legal personnel decisions on a regular basis—daily, or even hourly, in fact. And, there will be no problem because you are not making these decisions based on "protected class" status. There are only a few "protected classes" of employees, and we shall list them later on for you. Making decisions based on these "protected classes" can be illegal, but most of your decisions will be well within the parameters of the law.

Let's say that your unit is asked to send a representative up to the local college for a "career day" presentation. Your common sense tells you to send one of your college graduates up there to represent your department in front of those future college graduates. Are you discriminating against the non-college graduates of your unit? Maybe, if someone wants to state it that way. You made an administrative decision that is based on logic, common sense, and you have legitimate reasons to support your decision. Non-college graduates are not a "protected class" under the law. Your decision is legal and will withstand any legal challenge. But there is virtually no likelihood of there being one, since no "protected class" is involved in your decision.

In general, Title VII of the Civil Rights Act of 1964, and associated laws, define what a "protected class" is for employment purposes. These laws generally prohibit employment decisions that are based on race, color, religion, sex, age, national origin or disability. The nuances of the various laws are very detailed, and constantly in flux, and if you have a question, you should pose it in advance to your boss and/or your personnel department for clarification. But, in your daily activities, you should just be aware that based on your supervisory decisions involving any of these "protected class" distinctions can be legally questioned.

As an example, you must consider all your personnel as being of one ethnic group. You cannot send just white employees into white neighborhoods, nor only Hispanic employees into Hispanic neighborhoods. Ethnicity cannot, as a rule, be used as a basis for assignment or any other supervisory decisions.

Now the purpose of this chapter is not to make you an expert on civil rights law. The purpose is to give you a general awareness of the laws so that you don't make a bad supervisory decision. Our information should give you enough information that you have an "awareness" or warning flag to check further if you have any doubts. To that end, we shall give you a very brief overview of some of the "protected class" issues at hand. When in doubt, follow your organization's policies and procedure manual, and/or check with your personnel office or human resource contact before making a decision.

Discrimination (the basics): Discrimination against any protected class may include racial, ethnic or sexual slurs, segregation or harassment. Criminal justice agencies should take every precaution to ensure that such practices do not occur and if they do, that such practices will not be tolerated. This includes having written policies and procedures that address issues of discrimination. The policies should be distributed to all personnel and strictly enforced.

Sex discrimination (the basics): At least three Federal laws—Title VII of the Civil Rights Act of 1964, the Equal Pay Act of 1967, and the Pregnancy Discrimination Act—prohibit sex discrimination. In general, employers are required to ignore gender when hiring or promoting, provide equal pay and treat pregnancy the same as any other temporary medical disability. In any case involving such matters, contact your personnel office.

Sexual Harassment: The subject of sexual harassment will be discussed in a separate chapter in this book.

Religious Discrimination (the basics): This is a developing legal area. In general, employees who notify their employer of a conflict between employment practices and their religious beliefs are entitled to "a reasonable accommodation." That may include flexible scheduling, reassignment or lateral transfer. The bottom line is that if a conflict arises in your workplace involving a religious issue, you should immediately seek a written decision from your personnel office.

Discrimination based on national origin (the basics): "National origin" includes a person's place of origin *and* his or her ancestor's place of origin. You can see where this is going. Comments about Irish, Italian, English, Polish or any other country of origin or ethnicity are prohibited. That includes jokes and stereotypical comments, written or spoken. It can also be applied to anyone who speaks with an accent. Be aware and stop any such behavior before someone gets in trouble.

Discrimination based on disability (the basics): Although not generally an issue in criminal justice agencies at the supervisory level, you should be aware that the Americans with Disabilities Act does cover criminal justice agencies. You may encounter it more frequently if you supervise civilian personnel, although more and more sworn personnel fall under this category. If any issue arises, refer it immediately to your personnel office for resolution.

Discrimination based on age (the basics): The Age Discrimination and Employment Act (ADEA) makes it illegal to discriminate against persons forty years of age or older on the basis of their age. This should not be a problem for you as long as you don't make supervisory decisions based on age.

Discrimination based on race or color (the basics): You cannot make supervisory decisions based on an employee's race or color. And, you cannot allow racial slurs, segregation or harassment of any kind in your workplace. You are responsible for your employees' conduct.

Discrimination based on sexual orientation (the basics): Although not a specific Title VII issue, we believe it is best if you do not make any supervisory decisions based on sexual orientation. Nor should you allow any comments, slurs or harassment directed towards any sexual orientation or group. It's just good management practice, whether it is against the law or not. If it becomes an issue, let your personnel officer deal with it. They will know the most up-to-date state and federal laws on the subject.

We have given you a very brief overview of the major discrimination laws to make you aware of them. When in doubt, go to a higher, or more knowledgeable authority. Try your best to make good, sound decisions based on common sense and the issues at hand and you will do just fine.

What we have seen is too many criminal justice supervisors who are afraid to make decisions because it might offend someone. Well, unless that someone can prove that your decision was based unlawfully on their protected class status, your decision will stand.

Too many supervisors are intimidated by someone saying: "You're discriminating against me because I'm . . . (thin, fat, under-educated, married, not married, bald, short, tall, etc.)" Or . . . an employee who falls under one of the "protected classes" might say: "You only made that decision because I'm (fill in the blank)," when in reality, you made a decision based on performance, conduct or other objective criteria. You get the picture.

You know the laws, and have been to the seminars and training classes and know what "real" discrimination is, and you don't discriminate based on protected class status. So stand your ground and make your decisions based on the laws.

REVIEW QUESTIONS:

1. List 5 "protected classes" found under Title VII

2. Can ethnic jokes (i.e. Irish, Italian, Polish, etc.) be considered workplace discrimination? If so, what should you do in your role as a supervisor?

3. If a female employee advises you that she is pregnant, what should you do?

4. If one of your employees complains they object to a crucifix being displayed on another employee's desk, what should you do?

5. If an employee states that you are discriminating against him because he only has one car in the family and can't always get to work on time, what should you do?

CHAPTER 19

Sexual Harassment

So many criminal justice careers have been ruined by sexual harassment allegations, actions and court cases that we feel compelled to treat it as a separate chapter in this career development book. In one of the previous chapters of this book, we specifically told you that one of your duties as a criminal justice supervisor is to protect your people. Well, this chapter, best defined as "sexual harassment prevention," is your opportunity to protect your employees, yourself and your agency.

Your agency probably has already sent you to training seminars on sexual harassment prevention. And, of course, whatever they presented is the guideline to follow for your agency. Any, and all, questions should be referred to your personnel officer or legal counsel. Our work here is offered as a refresher to help you keep all your people out of trouble *before* an incident occurs.

Let's start with the basics: what is sexual harassment? Well, you won't find any law that says: "Thou shalt not sexually harass." However, sexual harassment has its roots in Title VII of the Civil Rights Act of 1964 (as amended), but the actual definition of sexual harassment is found in E.E.O.C. guidelines that generally have the force of law. At least that's what the legal people have told us over the years.

There are no separate standards for criminal justice personnel. But, in the interest of clarification and understanding, we would like to present our interpretation of the sexual harassment standards in a format that most criminal justice professionals can relate to. So, we have taken the standards and broken them into "elements," just as you might when looking at a criminal law. Let's take a look at the elements of burglary:

Burglary:
1. enters or remains
2. unlawfully
3. in a building

All three elements of the crime must be there to constitute the generic crime of burglary. Take away any of those elements, such as "unlawfully," and there is no burglary. Now that you know the general idea, here is our definition of the appropriate elements of sexual harassment:

Sexual harassment:
1. unwelcome
2. conduct
3. of a sexual nature
4. creating an intimidating, hostile or offensive working environment

Just as with the burglary example, all of the elements must be present to have sexual harassment. Take away any single element and it is no longer sexual harassment. Well . . . maybe it isn't! And, that creates all the problems. So much is often open to interpretation as to what constitutes sexual harassment and what constitutes, for example, "unwanted" as an element. In layman's terms, we will try to clarify things as best we can for you, but of course, the courts will always have the final say.

1. *Unwanted*—Who decides? Well, it is up to the recipient of the conduct to decide whether certain conduct is unwanted or not. One of the problems, from our viewpoint, is that the "give and take" of men and women working in the same environment may cross the legal line of sexual harassment—*if* it is interpreted as unwanted. And, what is viewed as good natured kidding today may be viewed as unwanted harassment tomorrow. Only the recipient knows for sure.

   (And do NOT try to excuse someone's errant behavior by saying something like: "We do this all the time!" That is not an excuse for their conduct, and in fact will only increase their culpability.)

2. *Conduct*—Go with the general legal definition that this can be any action. That includes speech, touch, even "leering" (although we have never found a really good legal definition of "leering"). But, one thing is very clear, if you eliminate the inappropriate conduct, you are well on your way to reducing or eliminating sexual harassment in your unit or workplace.

3. *Of a sexual nature*—Again, who decides if conduct is of a "sexual nature"? The recipient. The legal people may rule on it in the future, but initially, it is the recipient who makes that determination.

    The bright side is that this is perhaps the easiest element of sexual harassment to eliminate. Get all the "sex" out of the workplace and there is no sexual harassment. And, isn't that the intent of the law, anyway?

4. *Creating an intimidating, hostile or offensive working environment*—Guess who decides if this element is present or not? The recipient. And, without firm legal ground to counter this interpretation, the accused may have little chance to defend themselves.

Alright, those are the rules broken down in very basic terms (although we are sure that your agency's lawyer or human resource coordinator could be much more detailed and legal). But, that's the problem that you are facing in reducing or eliminating sexual harassment in your workplace. Some of your people just aren't professional enough (i.e., smart enough) to know what they should and should not do or say in today's litigious work environment. In fact, most of the cases where agencies and individuals are held financially liable result from essentially "rude and crude" behavior. That is not a legal definition, of course, but it is accurate. In fact, if we can eliminate all of the "rude and crude" conduct in the workplace, especially of a sexual nature, no doubt the vast majority of all sexual harassment complaints would cease.

And, that is one of the places where you (the boss) enter into this whole equation. You have a responsibility to attempt to prevent sexual harassment under your command. The first step is for you to know and implement your agency's sexual harassment policy. The legal standard that you will be held to is that you "knew or should have known" about sexual harassment in your workplace. You should continually monitor the interactions of your people, watch for any violations of your policy (there are no "misdemeanor" sexual harassment violations, every allegation is serious). You must take appropriate action when you observe any violations and then document your actions. As with other types of civil litigation, a sexual harassment lawsuit could be filed sometimes long after an incident, and the burden could be on you to prove what you did in your role as the boss.

Although your agency should provide adequate sexual harassment prevention training periodically, it may be up to you to be sure that your people know the policy and their own limitations from that policy. That may include your reiterating the policy at change of shift or a training meeting (which you might want to document). And, of course, you must stop any potential problems before they cross the line and place you, and your people, in a very difficult position.

Well, you might think that it seems easy—when the victim of a sexual harassment incident tells you about it, you will immediately spring into action and deal with the problem. However, often that is too late, and you could still be held accountable under the "knew or should have known" standard. The victim does not have to speak up at all. In fact, in some cases, they are afraid of the harasser or afraid they won't be believed, or afraid they won't be considered "one of the guys," or afraid of losing their jobs or remain silent for many other very legitimate reasons. These are "silent victims" and they need your protection. You should watch for symptoms of sexual harassment or intimidation. Take immediate action if you feel that your agency's policy has been violated. That way the victim is not the complainant . . . you are. If challenged by the offender that nobody is offended, make it clear that you are offended by the breach of policy.

Even allegations of sexual harassment in your unit or on your shift can cast a long shadow over your unit and your career for a long time. Even if such an allegation works its way through the system and is ultimately dismissed or unfounded or if one of your people is exonerated, there is still the lingering question of why there was an allegation in the first place. And, of course, if there is a determination or judgment that such sexual harassment did occur under your command, you may do well to escape with only a reprimand or demotion rather than a dismissal. Do not be surprised at this harsh reality. After all, you are responsible for the actions of your people and knew or should have known about such conduct under your command.

Again, we have put this layman's description of sexual harassment in this book because we have seen promising criminal justice professionals fired, demoted or seriously reprimanded for sexual harassment incidents. In this matter, you must take a firm stand, know and implement your policies, monitor conduct and document all of your training and actions taken consistent with your agency's policies. This is one critical area where you can fulfill your obligation to protect potential victims, the potential harasser, your department and your employer. And, most important of all, handling everything properly will protect your own career. Take sexual harassment seriously!

REVIEW QUESTIONS:

1. Why is sexual harassment so hard for you to define?

2. Cite the four "elements" of sexual harassment.

3. Who determines what is "unwelcome"?

4. What can you do to prevent sexual harassment?

CHAPTER 20

Coaching and Discipline

Most supervisors and most employees have the wrong idea about discipline. Almost everyone will immediately use the word "punishment" in defining this word, but take a minute to look up the definition in a dictionary. We did, and found five different definitions: ". . . training that develops self-control or orderliness and efficiency . . . a system of rules for the conduct of members . . . orderly conduct as a result of training . . . being subject to control . . . correction or punishment inflicted by way of correction or training." Only the last definition (the least important) mentions "punishment"

Discipline should **not** be considered punishment. It should encourage employees to meet certain standards of job performance. It is a form of training—although it may be on the extreme end of the training spectrum. Employees who meet or exceed expectations should be rewarded, while employees who cannot meet expectations should be trained, coached or counseled to motivate them and teach them necessary skills. Employees who cannot meet expectations after training, coaching and counseling should be disciplined.

We are convinced that most employees do not need disciplinary action. It should be used as a last resort, only after you have tried everything else. It should never be used by a boss as a show of authority or power. It should be used to assist an employee to correct faults that caused a problem, and help him continue with a positive attitude.

Positive discipline

This is not a contradiction. You can develop several options that can avoid the finality of punishment (negative discipline) by trying to prevent or limit potential problems.

1. *Have written standards in place*—Most employees do not object to policies and procedures or guidelines. Most are smart enough to know that if they follow the rules, they stay out of trouble. And, if they know what the rules are, they usually follow them. This is especially true if a supervisor takes the time to explain why the policies are in place, the value to the employee of following the policies and legal protections that the policies offer employees. When the group understands and accepts the policies, then sometimes minor infractions (either intentional ones or accidental ones) can be handled by the group (or the shift).

2. *Reasonable work objectives*—Most employees know what they "should" do, and if workloads are reasonable, and employees have a positive work environment, then the need for discipline will be drastically reduced. That's why Theory Y bosses have far fewer discipline problems than Theory X bosses.

3. *Supervisory example*—If you "lead by example," then others will follow. You create a very difficult work environment if you break the rules, then try to enforce them on your employees.

4. *Maintain uniformity in correcting behavior*—We like to use the "hot stove" example. Every time you touch a hot stove, it burns . . . and everyone gets burned the same when they touch the hot stove. The result (burning) is immediate, consistent and fair for everyone. That is the way discipline should be. If you have a written policy "not to touch the stove," and you train your employees "not to touch the stove," and you coach them "not to touch the stove," and then they touch the stove . . . what happens? They get penalized (but only *after* training and coaching).

   You have some discretion as a supervisor or boss, but use it in a very limited manner when it comes time to discipline. Your agency's policies and procedures (for major infractions) should be immediate, consistent and fair for everyone. Your own system (for minor infractions) should be the same.

5. *Eliminate causes that lead to misconduct*—Do you contribute to discipline problems as a boss? Do you under-supervise? Do you over-supervise? By ignoring the early warning signs, or minor infractions, you might be encouraging this and more serious behavior.

Positive discipline (that means avoiding or limiting discipline problems) can improve morale, reduce egregious behavior, can cause you less headaches as a boss, and make your job a lot easier. Seems like a "no-brainer" to us!

Negative discipline

This means the various alternatives that criminal justice agencies and bosses have to correct behavior problems by penalizing the offending employee. (Of course, each criminal justice agency has different policies, different contracts, different unions, different state laws, etc.)

Negative discipline in private sector jobs is much different than public sector—criminal justice—jobs. Anyone who has ever worked in the private sector knows that sometimes employees don't know they are being disciplined until the boss calls them into the office and fires them, or you come in to work in the morning and your co-worker is missing. In criminal justice, the influence of civil service, unions, strong contracts, grievances and state laws often make serious discipline more complex.

You may have very limited authority as a supervisor to impose discipline, and it is *critical* that you know how much authority you do have. Do you know what your contract says? Do you know what your policies say? Do you know what your state personnel laws say? Sometimes you do not have time to guess or look it up.

In any situation that involves discipline, use facts, not feelings. The value of documentation is *critical*. Arbitrators rely on documented progressive discipline. Make sure you know what you are doing before you do it.

Reasons for NOT disciplining employees

No supervisor *likes* to discipline their people, but the professional bosses do what needs to be done. Because these situations can become contentious, they can be legally challenged, and it makes all parties involved very uncomfortable. Poor bosses tend to avoid this difficult task. Why?

One research study done on this topic showed the top five reasons for NOT disciplining employees. Be honest—see if you have used any of these as an excuse.

1. *Not documenting previous incidents*—43% of supervisors responded that they failed to begin the paper trail.

2. *No support from management*—40% of supervisors responded that they didn't bother because they did not believe that their actions would be supported from above.

3. *Supervisor does not know the rules*—29% of supervisors responded to this. Poor supervisors figure that it's better to do nothing than do something and have it be wrong.

4. *The employee is a close friend of the supervisor*—20% of supervisors said that they felt uncomfortable disciplining a friend. Well, remember the "hot stove" that we mentioned earlier? What do you think this lack of action does to the morale, motivation and respect of the other employees? It is very difficult for a boss to rebuild the damage done by inconsistent discipline.

5. *Supervisor wants to be a good guy*—18% of the bosses responded to this one. Of course, we all want to be liked. That is an important part of our human make-up. But, as a supervisor, if you have a choice between being "liked" or being "respected" by your subordinates, choose being respected. It's nice to have both, but we will take employees' respect anytime over popularity.

REVIEW QUESTIONS

1. Why do most supervisors and most employees have the wrong idea about discipline?

2. What is the purpose of discipline?

3. Why is "positive discipline" important?

4. What are some critical issues that supervisors need to be aware of in regards to negative discipline?

5. What are five reasons given by supervisors for not disciplining employees?

CHAPTER 21

Personnel Evaluations

Measuring and evaluating a subordinate's performance can be a very challenging task for any supervisor or administrator, regardless of how long they have been in that position. One of the biggest problems is that many criminal justice agencies are small and you work with the same people every day, often for years. In fact, you may be an employee in a small criminal justice agency today and be promoted in that same agency tomorrow. That can create all kinds of potential problems for you. The "good news-bad news" is that you know your people very well (including all their screw-ups, mistakes, problems and personal weaknesses). And, the "good news-bad news" is that they know you very well, too (including all of your screw-ups, mistakes, problems and personal weaknesses).

Most professional criminal justice agencies have a personnel evaluation system in place. And many people involved (employees, supervisors and administrators) view evaluations as a pain in the neck. Often supervisors half-heartedly fill out the forms. Sometimes they may be required to meet with the employee to "discuss" their evaluations (which often amounts to the supervisor saying to the employee: "Here is your evaluation form. Sign it and I'll give you a copy. Any questions?"). After that, it's all forgotten for another year.

Of course, a worse case scenario occurs in criminal justice agencies that do not have any formal evaluation process. In these cases, the employee tries his/her best to stay out of trouble, wonders what they are doing right (usually because no one ever bothers to tell them), and knows exactly when they do something wrong (because the boss is always there to criticize).

If your agency has an evaluation system in place, then re-read the policies and procedures so that you are familiar with the process, both from an employee's role and a supervisor's role. Follow your own agency's personnel evaluation system and guidelines. Here, we only present generic guidelines for guidance only.

Benefits of performance evaluations

There are several important benefits of having written evaluations done on every employee, regardless of rank.

- *Evaluations ensure that work standards are met.* They can keep you and your employees out of trouble. They also measure an employee's performance against established job requirements. This is especially important when it comes time to discipline or fire an employee.

- *Evaluations provide employees with feedback.* It can eliminate excuses from poor performers because evaluations let every employee know exactly where they stand. It also recognizes one of our basic human needs—recognition. Many employees do lots of good work that can tend to be forgotten or overlooked, until they screw-up . . . then ZAP! All the good work is forgotten. Well, a good evaluation system looks at 12 months of work (usually) and recognizes the good and the not-so-good for the entire time period.

- *Evaluations can also identify training needs.* They can provide a basis for employee development and training. Specific problems with individual employees can be identified (poor report writing, low productivity, poor courtroom testimony skills, etc.), and too many similar problems may show that several employees have similar training needs, and the agency can then plan accordingly.

- *Evaluations become part of a permanent employee record.* This tracking should not be viewed as a negative, because (when properly used . . .) evaluations can be used to track good performance as well. And, of course, evaluations should track the performance of marginal employees, After all, what happens to morale among the "A" players when supervisors ignore mediocre work or do not recognize outstanding work?

Common rating errors

For several reasons supervisors can fall into certain habits that must be avoided for an evaluation system to have any meaning. Sometimes these supervisory mistakes are based on a lack of "performance evaluation training," while in other cases, it is based on a supervisor's attempt to have the employees "like" them. Either way, see if any of these problems sound too familiar to you.

- *Leniency*—This is the most common rating error! Employees are given higher marks than they actual deserve. This is sometimes done by supervisors to avoid conflict or confrontation. After all, a lot of employees "like" a lenient boss.

  Of course, this creates several serious problems. First, a rater has nowhere to go if the employee's performance improves. Also, it is difficult to motivate an employee to improve when he is getting high marks for mediocrity. In addition, this error may backfire on the supervisor through litigation if the employee gets sued for poor judgment or behavior and the supervisor knew about it but failed to document it properly.

- *Personal bias*—We all tend to like some people more than others. Perhaps we like the same sports team, or have similar personalities, or whatever. But, you can't afford to "like" one of your employees more than another when it comes time to evaluate them. You have to focus on performance, not "likes." Likes and dislikes limit your objectivity as a supervisor.

  This can create serious problems for a supervisor. A "like" or "dislike" towards a subordinate tends to be very obvious to everyone else. This can cause serious morale problems on your shift. Once this occurs, it destroys your credibility and effectiveness as a supervisor. It can also set you up for lawsuits and/or grievances. Many harassment and discrimination grievances are filed as a result of favoritism or unequal treatment by the supervisor.

- *Central grouping*—This occurs when a supervisor groups all their employees in the middle. This is often done if the supervisor must justify extremely high or low ratings (which involves more paperwork for lazy supervisors). It is often done because it can be the "easy way out" for non-confrontational supervisors. It eliminates telling one employee they are better or worse than others, it does not require specific documentation and is often done for last-minute or hurried evaluations.

  Of course, this creates serious problems for supervisors, too. Employees will soon begin to feel that you don't care about them, and if you don't care, why should they? Employees do compare evaluations and if the better employees are lumped together with the mediocre employees, what incentive is there for the better employees to keep being motivated? This will quickly and certainly create an entire shift of mediocre or average employees. Kind of a self-fulfilling prophecy for the poor supervisor.

- *Halo effect*—This occurs when a supervisor allows one or two traits to dominate the entire evaluation. Sometimes ratings are done on general impressions rather than a specific trait (e.g., "He takes good care of his uniform so he must be an above-average employee," or "She is a good people-person, so I'll rate her above average overall."). Sometimes this occurs when the supervisor and the employee share similar backgrounds, job interests or hobbies (e.g., a similar "like" for DWI arrests, public speaking, criminal investigations, etc.). Often a supervisor who is a good criminal investigator may overrate a police officer who is a good criminal investigator, even though she may be deficient in other areas.

  Once again, this creates problems for the supervisor. It gives a false sense of performance for the employee, especially when they get transferred to another shift or when you get transferred and they get another supervisor to rate them. This problem also does not give proper feedback to the employee in the areas that they may be weak in so that they might improve those areas. And, of course, this is another fault that can destroy the credibility of the best rating system in only a few years,

- *Overweighting*—Lazy supervisors tend to remember events that occur at the end of the rating period best, and this can slant the entire year, whether the events are good or bad. An evaluation system that does not allow for proper documentation during the entire rating period may allow this fault to happen. Good supervisors track their employees' performance all the time, and whether the agency has a proper documentation process or not, these good supervisors have accurate records to document both the positive and the negative.

- *Severity*—Some supervisors give low marks on evaluations because of personal biases or beliefs not related to actual performance. Perhaps you have heard a boss say something like this: "No one gets 'outstanding' because no one walks on water" or "If I give him an 'outstanding', then he won't be able to improve next year." This, of course, doesn't make much sense. It would be the equivalent of a teacher making it impossible for a student to get 100% on a test. If the mark cannot be achieved, then why bother having it?

  This creates some serious problems for supervisors. You can see how the better employees would lose motivation very quickly. Also, this can lead to a very inconsistent picture of the performance of an employee between two raters. And, this problem certainly discourages any effort to improve performance by employees.

Sources of information for evaluations

There are many sources that you should consult in gathering objective and, if necessary, legally defensible data for your employees' evaluations.

General departmental sources:

1. *Attendance records*—Sick time, vacation, training days, special assignments, etc.

2. *Statistics*—BEWARE! Statistics can be devastating on employee motivation if used improperly. For example, if Officer Jones writes 30 traffic tickets a month and Officer Smith writes 15 traffic tickets a month, does that mean that Officer Jones is twice as good as Officer Smith, or works twice as hard? What about the quality of the tickets? What if Officer Smith had several days of sick leave and several days of training and was only on patrol duty half the days that Officer Jones worked? A good supervisor has the answers to these questions (and others) BEFORE he puts anything in writing.

3. *Complaints*—Some agencies actually consider the number of personnel complaints as part of the evaluation process. Of course, employees who never do anything will never do anything wrong, so they don't have any complaints written on them. But, often, the energetic, motivated and high-producing employee may have several complaints filed against them (perhaps all of them unfounded). Which is the "better" employee? Who should be rated higher?

4. *Personnel folders*—A lot of work that employees do in the course of a year does not always get into their personnel folder. But, good supervisors look at the commendations, training records, "atta boy" letters from citizens, etc., that may end up there. Added to this information is personal data that could be included. For example, is the employee going to night school, does he/she have a special skill that could be developed, should specific training be recommended?

Other specific sources of information that supervisors might consider:

1. *Report writing*—Some supervisors track the report writing abilities of their employees by maintaining an individual tally sheet for reports submitted by each employee; one column for the number submitted, one column for

the number approved without corrections, one column for reports returned once, etc. It makes for additional work for the supervisor, but this type of documentation may be critical when you are legally challenged for an evaluation that you wrote.

2. *Productivity*—Every criminal justice agency has some means of measuring the amount of work that an employee generates. But, don't look at statistics without weighing certain tasks to reflect what is important to the agency or the unit that you work in. For example, the quantity of traffic tickets versus the quality of the tickets, the number of arrests compared with the number of cases that the district attorney does not prosecute the number of self-activated arrests, etc.

3. *Appearance and attitude*—Observe all your employees for appropriate appearance. Are their clothes clean and pressed, are their shoes shined? Do they look "professional"? And, along with their appearance, what about their attitude and demeanor? How do they interact with clients, the citizens and each other. Listen to your employees as they handle the day-to-day activities that they perform. Do they sound like "professionals"?

4. *Individual employee log sheet*—Most evaluations are done on a yearly basis. To be fair, supervisors need to maintain regular documentation on their subordinates' performance—good and bad. We have found that by maintaining a "performance log sheet" on each employee, this fairly and accurately monitors their performance for the entire time of the evaluation period (as opposed to only remembering the bad screw-ups or the most recent incidents). Whether your agency has a formal evaluation system or not, this is a great way to show that you want to document each of your employee's performance. This log sheet should contain notes on performance, any documentation, any information that a supervisor observes during the evaluation period—the good and the bad. This works best when employees know about it (this is NOT a "black book"), and in fact,

employees should have the option to review this log sheet anytime. These should not be secret, but of course, they should be kept secure. Don't trust your memory—make regular entries. Review the folder at the end of each evaluation period, then destroy the contents and begin again.

Conclusion

Many evaluation systems that criminal justice agencies have in place now will become ineffective after a few years. Think about the evaluation process that you have in your agency. Is it viewed as a positive? Do employees "grow" from these evaluations? Are the evaluations viewed as learning tools, and a chance for dialogue between the employees and their supervisor? Or are evaluations viewed as a bother, an inconvenience, an awkward moment where supervisors and employees roll their eyes with dread?

Why do evaluation systems fail? For many of the reasons we have just listed. Evaluations will work only if the administration, the supervisors and the employees view them as a positive learning tool. Evaluations will only work if all of the supervisors agree among themselves to avoid the rating errors that we are all prone to make, and rate each employee fairly and objectively. One of the main reasons why evaluation systems fail is because of lack of training for the people who are involved in the evaluation system, especially the supervisors. How many of you have received rater training specific to the evaluation system that you have in your agency? Do your part to help make your evaluation system do what it is supposed to do.

REVIEW QUESTIONS:

1. Why is measuring and evaluating a subordinate's performance a very challenging task for any supervisor or administrator, regardless of how long they have been in that position?

2. What are the benefits of having a formal evaluation system in place in a criminal justice agency?

3. Describe the most common rating errors that supervisors have.

4. List some specific sources of information/data that can be used to prepare an objective performance evaluation.

5. What can supervisors do to improve the effectiveness of their agencies' performance evaluation system?

CHAPTER 22

Time Management

How much of your day revolves around time? Whether it is trying to remember what time you are supposed to pick the kids up, or checking the clock to see if it is time to go to work, or (for many of us) looking forward to what time we get out of work, we spend a great deal of our personal and professional life revolving around a very abstract thing called "time."

Why is it that time seems to pass so quickly when we are on our days off, or when we are approaching a deadline to finish a big project at work, yet time passes so slowly when we are working midnight shift and trying to stay alert at 4:00 a.m., or when we are on a boring surveillance assignment. Time is a funny thing.

We all do our best to manipulate time. Some people drive faster than the speed limit to try and "pick up a few minutes," or use a drive-thru window at a fast food restaurant to "save a few minutes," or color their hair to "turn back the clock." Of course, we are all fooling ourselves. Time marches on at a measured and precise pace that we have no control over.

One interesting concept about time is that it is fair to every person. We all are given the same amount of time to use every day—sixty seconds in a minute, sixty minutes in an hour, etc. Obviously, we cannot control time, but what we can learn to do is "manage" time. Usually, successful people in any profession have had to overcome the "time" problem. The more successful you become in your criminal justice career, the more people expect of you, the more responsibility you are given and the more important it will become to manage your time.

Getting the most out of your time

You can't control time . . . you can't stop time . . . you can't wish for more time . . . the only choice you have in your hectic day is to manage the time that you have.

There are many "time management" books in the business section of your local bookstore. We admit that we have not read them all (. . . we don't have the "time"!) But, what we can do is offer you some ideas that might work for you to better organize your professional life.

For example, one of the most basic time management ideas is to make a "to do" list at the end of each day of the things that you need to do tomorrow. It is incredibly simple (in fact some modern-day "gurus" scoff at this and call this "first-generation time management"), but . . . it works. At the end of each business day, just take out a slip of paper and plan ahead for tomorrow. List the things that are important for you to do and then prioritize the list. The "A's" are the highest priority, "B's" are medium and "C's" are lowest. When your next work day begins, focus on the "A" list, and as things come across your desk, unless it is MORE important than the "A" task you are working on, merely place that new task somewhere on the "B" or "C" list and focus back on the "A" task. I know . . . easier said than done, but . . . you have to learn new habits and begin to manage your time better.

This simple "to do" list is a good place to start. (Call me old-fashioned, but I use a "to do" list almost every day. As I complete a certain task, I cross it off my list using a red pen. It gives me a sense of accomplishment at the end of my day to see red lines across my list. And if I did not complete enough tasks . . . and I don't see enough red lines, it reinforces my need to better focus tomorrow and eliminate the distractions that prevented me from completing my list today.) Once you get the idea of a daily "to-do" list, then you can begin to plan for a weekly "to-do" list or a monthly "to-do" list. However, we have found that the long-range goals and tasks often take care of themselves if you include smaller jobs in your daily list. For example, if you have to complete a grant application by the end of the month, it would be foolish to wait until the last day of the month to fill it out. So, a priority on your "to-do" list today might be to complete "Section A" of the grant application, and next Monday, your "to-do" list priority would be to complete Section B, etc.

Stuff . . .

So how do you stay focused on your immediate priority tasks when "stuff" keeps getting thrown at you? You know the "stuff" we are referring to . . . the phone rings, one of your employees wants to see you for a minute, you have about ten e-mails that need to be handled, paperwork is piling up in your in-basket, there are some things that you should have done but have been putting off doing, etc.

Let's start with some ideas on handling the ever-growing amount of paperwork that crosses your desk every day.

First, if in doubt, throw it out. Lots of people send you lots of "stuff" that they think you care about. Well, you don't! Here is a good rule to follow: "If in doubt, throw it out." If you can avoid getting things sent to you, do it. And, another idea is that if you are on an agency's routing slip and every document, every report piece and every piece of paper is automatically sent to you, then ask that your name be taken off the routing slip and that only information critical for your current job ends up in your in-basket.

Second, a lot of us are on e-mail lists for different electronic documents, internal e-mails, even "guess who is having a birthday today" e-mails (No . . . we don't make this stuff up!), etc. Unless you REALLY need to receive e-mails from other people, ask to be taken off their e-mail lists. It's stuff we really don't care about, we really don't need and it really takes up our time sorting through it.

Next, one of the more famous laws of business is: "Clutter expands to fill the amount of space available for its retention." A basic organizational idea for your office is to have one SMALL place on your desk for your work. For example, one small in-basket is all you should allow yourself for pending work, or one small stack of file folders for your work in progress. You cannot allow yourself to accumulate more "stuff" than that. This one small space forces you to deal with clutter as it comes in.

Avoid doing your more difficult administrative work at times when you know that you are going to be busy. When I used to work in law enforcement, I used to avoid working dayshift for a couple of different reasons, but one of these reasons was that there were always too many distractions going on for me to focus for any length of time. When I had to work day shift, I would come in an hour early and close my office door, or stay an hour late. It's amazing how much work you can do when people don't know you are around!

Another idea that works for a lot of people is to perform related duties and tasks all at the same time. For example, open all your e-mails and respond to them first thing in the morning, or answer your correspondence all at the same time, or if you have to see several of your employees during the day, try to arrange these visits one after the other rather than randomly spaced out during the day.

Lastly, figure out when you have the most energy during the day and plan on tackling your most important tasks then. Do not waste this high-energy time on routine tasks like responding to e-mails.

Your biggest time-wasters

As a supervisor, administrator, manager or someone who works in an office setting, you are continually battling the need to "save" time and avoid "wasting" time. Let us list a couple of the most common time-wasters and how you can quickly yet effectively deal with them.

1. *Meetings.* How many hours a week do you spend at meetings? It seems that the higher up you go, the more meetings you are expected to attend. They all seem important to the person who called the meeting, and you MUST be important because you are on the list of people called to the meeting. But how many of these meetings are poorly planned, don't start on time, wander off the agenda, have no clear objectives, have people invited who have no real reason to be there, and have no one in charge?

   Meetings should be called as a last resort, not as an obligatory social function. The list of people invited should be as short as possible. You need to take charge of the meeting and not let someone else direct where the meeting is going. Do some pre-meeting contacts with key people so they are informed about what is going on. They may help you move an item on the agenda quickly rather than having to schedule another meeting. Why is it that there is ALWAYS food and drinks at meetings? Wouldn't things move along faster if you spent more time talking and less time eating? Here's another great idea (at least I think so . . .). If you want to have short meetings, don't have chairs at your meeting. People will get a lot more work done more quickly when they are uncomfortable.

2. *Telephone calls/cell phones/e-mails.* I lump these all together because you can spend a LOT of time getting very little "A" tasks done when you spend time on these "C" tasks. These are wonderful inventions, but . . . they have turned into our adult umbilical cords. I know that we think we all are very important people, but when you are trying to focus on a critical "A" task, you really don't need the interruptions that these three inventions give us too many times every day.

   If you have problems with these interruptions, then the obvious solution is to cut your adult umbilical cord, at least temporarily. Most of the interruptions from these three sources can wait. You have NO real reason—except a bad habit—to immediately answer the ring or the "boing" (at least that is the sound my computer makes when I receive an e-mail). Can you wait until your coffee break to return these calls? Can you wait until you are on your way to or from your office to return the calls? Can you wait until lunch time or the last couple of minutes of your shift? We ALL act like Pavlov's dogs when we hear the ring or the "boing"—let's try controlling technology instead of having technology control us.

3. *Walk-ins*—You have all heard that good bosses have an "open door policy" for their employees. "Come on in . . . I always have time to talk to you." Well . . . forget it— you don't always have time! That's maybe why you are having problems with time management. Unexpected emergencies are one thing—they do come up in criminal justice—but it is the random "walk-in" that can break

your chain of thought, interrupt your work and generally kill too much of your precious time.

Some solutions may be really obvious—close your office door (if you have a door)—make it clear that you are busy when they say, "Got a minute?"—let your employees know ahead of time that you are working on a major project. Drop a loud hint that you get your best work done between 8 and 10 (or whenever your high-energy, most motivated time of your day is). When a bored subordinate or bored peer tries to take up your time (because they have nothing to do), ask them in a nice way (of course) "Gee, if you need something to do, I can find something for you." That will clear them out fast!

4. *Socializing/gossip*—We all like to socialize. It is part of our human nature. However, there is a big difference between effective group dynamics around the coffee pot or around the office and time-wasting, negative and destructive office gossip. Don't lock yourself away from the idle chatter, the friendly give-and-take, and the necessary interaction between bosses and employees. But, realize that this can cross over into negative, back-stabbing and destructive gossip pretty quickly.

One of the best ways to avoid getting trapped in the cycle of time-wasting office gossip is to make it clear that a few minutes of idle chatter about the ball game or a subordinates' family or whatever is acceptable, but then a simple, "Let's get back to work," will set the tone for what you expect of yourself and others. It won't take long for your subordinates to take the hint. If not, then you can always make the hint a little more direct next time.

REVIEW QUESTIONS

1. Why is time "fair" to every person?

2. What are the advantages of making a "to-do" list?

3. What are five ways of dealing with the "Stuff" that crosses your desk every day?

4. What are four of your biggest time-wasters and how can you effectively deal with each of these?

CHAPTER 23

Decision Making

The work of being a boss involves the job of solving problems. The work of being a *successful* boss involves the job of solving problems *successfully*. Employees don't have problems—they have supervisors! (Although sometimes supervisors are the problem!)

Remember "the old days' as an entry-level employee? It was so easy . . . all you had to do was keep your nose clean, stay out of trouble, avoid seeing the boss, and go home at the end of your shift. It was easy taking care of you! Not now. If you have six employees working for you, it seems that you have six people trying to get you in trouble . . . if you have fifty people working for you, it seems you have fifty people trying to get you in trouble! Maybe it is the burden of increasingly more responsibility, or the over-reaction to vicarious liability, or perhaps you are dealing with lesser-trained personnel. Whatever the reasons, it may seem that being a successful boss today seems a lot more difficult than in "the old days"! However, in reality, successful bosses (who are successful decision-makers) have always had certain things in common.

Start with a plan

You are a problem solver! But remember that problems are not always bad. Some problems result merely from change (and what criminal justice agency out there isn't changing!). Change can be viewed as a negative or a positive. Most people perceive change as negative because "change" disrupts their normal status quo. Most of us (most employees) prefer neat and predictable lives . . . whether on the job or at home. Maybe a good basic definition of a problem is: a gap between what you expect and what really is. On the job, this can translate into many, many different scenarios, and *you* are somehow responsible to make them all right!

To do it right, decision-making involves choosing a course of action from *perceived and available* alternatives in order to achieve a desired goal. (Obviously, we highlighted this phrase for a reason that we will talk about later.)

Developing a track record of making good decisions consistently involves a process. It is not like throwing darts with your eyes closed. (Although sometimes it can be a lot like throwing a hand grenade—sometimes if you are close to the right decision, it turns out okay.) We highlighted the terms "perceived and available alternatives" to remind you that perception often becomes reality. Too many poor decisions have been made based on a preconceived decision, in spite of what available information says, rather than gathering available information first, then making a decision.

Steps in the decision-making process

Here's one way of learning to make good decisions:

1. *Define the problem*—How is the situation you're looking at different than "normal"? Is the problem real or perceived (ex: sometimes rumors can create problems). Is it **your** problem to solve? (ex: some employees may try to "give" you a problem that is really theirs to solve.) How widespread is the problem? If it appears overwhelming to you, break the problem into parts and establish priorities for solving each part of the problem. If there are multiple problems, is there a common denominator that can be addressed (ex: if all the supervisors are complaining about spending too much time doing paperwork, maybe the common problem is poor report writing skills on the part of the employees.)

2. *Gather as many of the facts as possible*—This may sound incredibly obvious, but how many bosses have you worked for that "fired first and asked questions later." They jumped to conclusions, made assumptions, got half the story, then fired off their decision . . . only to regret being too jumpy later on. Now, because many decisions

we make in criminal justice need quick and decisive decision-making, you may not be able to gather **all** the information, but be sure to gather as much relevant information as possible, and be objective and thorough in your analysis.

3. *Determine possible alternatives*—Every problem has at least two choices. Be sure to evaluate the consequences of each choice. How will each choice change the situation? What undesirable outcomes could each choice have? Don't be afraid to brainstorm with your employees or peers or people who have more knowledge of an issue than you, if you have time. (Of course, you are still ultimately responsible and accountable for the decision.)

4. *Decide the best alternative*—Using logic, common sense and all available relevant information to choose the best alternative. Remember, many decisions you will have to make will be made under less than ideal conditions, therefore your decision may be less than ideal, but . . . you still have to make the call. Also, the best thought-out plan can change quickly, so have an alternative plan of action available, just in case. (You have all heard of Murphy's Law.)

5. *Schedule a plan of action*—Give a thorough explanation and guidance to all those involved in your decision. Obviously, make sure they have the resources, training and abilities to carry your plan of action to a successful conclusion. Plan out possible obstacles to your decision (be your own "enemy" and try and shoot down your plan like your opponents might). Feedback is critical in the planning and decision-making process. Be sure you are getting enough accurate and unbiased feedback from all involved parties.

Two types of problems

Basically, there are two types of problems that you will face as a boss: job-related problems, and people-related problems.

1. *Job-related problems*—These directly affect how you and your employees do the job. The small problems that come at you daily should be disposed of in an orderly and consistent manner without too much effort. Don't let small problems build up—make a decision and move on.

    How about this idea—learn to solve these small problems in forty-five seconds. 1. Mentally re-state the problem and review the facts (15 seconds); 2. Weigh your alternatives and choose the best one. Make a decision now! (20 seconds) and; 3. Announce your decision and make sure that the recipients understand it and can execute it (10 seconds).

    Do not let small problems accumulate!

    Now major job-related problems could have a long-lasting effect on operations. They may change the existing status quo and may have side effects that need to be considered. These deserve more careful consideration. Slow down.

    For these more serious problems, avoid making quick, snap decisions. Get as many facts as possible. Ask questions, like: What has been done before? What worked? Why didn't previous decisions work? What is the "real" source of the problem? (ex.: high usage of sick leave does not always mean it is flu season!) Don't hesitate to consult with others, even if you do not "like" them or if you already know you do not agree with what they have to say. (ex: the union president in your criminal justice agency may have some valid reasons why sick leave usage is so high—but, some bosses don't want to hear the truth!)

2. *People-related problems*—Often these are far more complicated and very different than job-related problems. Sometimes people-problems arise from job problems, but more often come from the fact that we have to hire people to work for us. And, they all have feelings, emotions, perceptions, different goals, and various other human weaknesses and frailties.

    Sometimes, simple people-problems come from

employees looking for special requests or special treatment. ("Boss, can I leave work about thirty minutes early tonight? I have to pick my kids up from day-care early.") These may not seem important on the grand scale of the overall operations of your agency or shift, but they are often **very** important to the individual employee.

Some of these simple decisions can be made by answering the following two questions:

1. Is there a policy to cover the request? If so, use it, and carefully explain why and what you are using to base your decision on. (In the above example, the explanation might be: "Sure you can leave work thirty minutes early. Be sure to fill out a time slip to use thirty minutes of comp. time. You know, I can't let you out early without documenting your absence." That should cover it, without any questions or comments from your employees. Pretty straightforward!)

2. Will granting this request hurt your relationship with other employees? Could your decision be viewed as "special treatment"? If so, don't allow it, and state your reasons clearly. (In the previous example, if the employee complains about . . . "why do I need to fill out a slip for only thirty minutes. What's the big deal?") You know that if you let one employee "get away" with bending the rules, then **all** your employees are going to want to break the rules.

Sometimes, people problems exist between employees and are more complicated than the previous "easy" example. Sometimes these may involve only one employee. (Ex: One of your better employee's productivity is down. How long do you let it go without saying something? How do you open the conversation when you do approach it?) Sometimes, two or more employees are in conflict in their workplace. These problems can affect employee morale, productivity and the overall dynamics of your shift or your role as a supervisor. Any of these can create serious problems for you.

If you have a problem involving two employees who are in conflict, here are some ideas for your plan of action:

1. Listen fairly to both sides without taking sides. This is often hard to do, especially if you view one of the parties involved as a "whiner."
2. Look beyond the information they give you. Perhaps each of them is being less than honest with you, and may withhold certain information. Look for the hidden agenda that each may have.
3. Weigh all the facts. Make a fair decision. And, even though one party will not think your decision is right, at least they should think it was done fairly.
4. Communicate your decision to all parties firsthand. Take the time to personally deliver your decision. To do less might indicate that you are hesitant to confront your employees.
5. Follow up and do what you can to restore and rebuild the damage done to relationships involved in your decision.

Sometimes you have to be a little creative in making decisions. For example, we knew of one manager who was making a very difficult decision about consolidating dispatch services in a criminal justice agency. There was one particular sergeant who was very vocal about his opposition to the plan. In a stroke of genius, or perhaps it was a bold move by the manager to realize that he might have missed something in making this decision, the boss put the responsibility of implementing the decision in the hands of the sergeant. Now some people might call this risky, or foolish, but it worked. The sergeant implemented the plan, gained a much better understanding of all of the issues involved, and with that additional knowledge, openly admitted later on that he was wrong to oppose the plan initially.

Another example of making a risky people-related

decision involved two police officers who really, *really*, *really* did not get along. This became bad for the morale of the entire shift, as they continually took "shots" at each other, and were splitting the shift into two "camps" depending on who the other officers supported. It became so bad that morale, motivation and productivity on that shift dropped dramatically, and the sergeant on that shift was transferred because he did not handle the problem. (This incident adversely affected his career later on.) The new sergeant who came in dealt with the problem very quickly. He made both of the officers patrol car partners. He told them: "I can't make you like each other, but I can make you work together." It was risky, but it worked. They never did become friends, but they learned to respect each other and treated each other like professionals.

Conclusion

Maintain your perspective! Most of your decisions will fall into the "normal" range. You will win some and you will lose some. You will not be right every time. If you know anything about the bell-shaped curve, you will know that out of ten decisions that you will make, two will be great, two will be wrong, and the rest will fit into the "acceptable" range, that no one will know or care much about.

As you make more and more decisions, and as these decisions become more and more important as you move up the career ladder, remember to leave room for error—your errors, and the errors of your employees. We are all human enough to make mistakes. Good employees (and good bosses) learn from their mistakes.

A few problems will take up the majority of your time. Be prepared for this by dealing with the everyday, minor problems quickly and efficiently. This clears you to focus on the most serious problems that need the most attention.

Remember that every decision that you make involves risk. It cannot be avoided. Any decision can be wrong, but not making a decision is **always** wrong! Expect risk, but you can minimize it by having a logical, problem-solving plan in place.

REVIEW QUESTIONS:

1. What steps are there in the decision-making process?

2. Define the two types of decisions that supervisors typically are involved in.

3. What are some of the issues that supervisors need to consider in making "people-related" decisions?

CHAPTER 24

Risk Management

Since you chose to enter a career in criminal justice, we know that you have a solid level of both moral and physical courage. You likely have a good sense of what is right and what is wrong. And, you are likely to use your own physical and mental abilities to help honesty and law triumph over dishonesty and crime. And, for that type of moral dedication, you are a tribute to the criminal justice community.

In an ideal world, we would make laws, enforce them with sound policies and make all of our decisions within those guidelines. Everyone would comply with the rules and life would be good. So good that we wouldn't need supervisors or command personnel because everyone would always do the right thing under all circumstances. In fact, we wouldn't need a criminal justice system at all in this Utopia.

Now, return to the real world and the realities of crime and the criminal justice system. Laws are open to individual judgments and interpretation, police and prosecutors exercise discretion in the enforcement of laws and the prosecution of offenders. Politics and economics can thwart the good intentions of many people in the criminal justice system. The system CAN work, and generally does, but not always.

So where do you, and more importantly your career, stand in all of this uncertainty? You swore to uphold the laws and the Constitution when you took your oath of office. But, where are you going to stand when the "right" road is blurred by the fog of real world influences? What will you do when you are sworn to enforce the laws, but your people are outnumbered 100 to 1 by an angry and violent mob? What will you do when the mayor, your boss, tells you to "look the other way" in an ongoing corruption scandal? What will you do when your internal affairs investigation pits you against some of your best employees or close friends? And these are just some of the 'risk management' situations you may face during your criminal justice career.

Okay, it is not our job to create problems for you, it is our job to help you deal with potential problems in your career, hopefully before you reach them. In fact, we want to help you avoid problems, or be prepared for them if they confront you. When it comes to risk management for your career, either physical or political, we want you to be prepared to handle the situation. So here it goes. We hope you can follow us as we address this sensitive, and sometimes controversial subject.

Risk management is about balancing the potential cost versus the potential benefit in a given situation. We will start out with the simple "unruly crowd" example. A crowd is large and unhappy and is protesting a 'police brutality incident' that the press has focused on. They commit violations of the law, such as blocking the streets, burning the flag and some wooden picnic tables and park benches. You have a single shift of police officers—twelve to be exact. Are you going to order your twelve police officers to wade into a group of hundreds of angry protestors? Or will you delay and call for backup from the county sheriff, state police, fire department and off-duty personnel? If you wade into the crowd to enforce the law, you are very likely to have officers seriously injured. And, even if you arrest the ringleaders, what will you do with them? You could lose a couple of officers for each person you arrest while they transport the arrested subjects for processing. And, that's all discounting what will appear on the 6 o'clock news. Will police use of force be seen as solidifying some of the community's perception of police brutality? Yet, if you standby and wait for backup, crowd control teams, special tactics teams, etc., and the crowd escalates and causes more damage, you may be blamed for your lack of action. It's not so simple anymore, is it?

So, how much risk are you willing to take? How many, and to what degree, are you willing to risk your people? One instance of placing them at unreasonable risk will label you as a bad commander for the rest of your career, yet not quickly responding to a situation will also label you. Lose a battle (. . . you don't get paid to lose battles) and your credibility is gone. Embarrass the police chief and the politicians, and you will be looking for a new job. But, hesitate to 'go into battle' and you will be viewed as weak and indecisive.

Only you can decide how much risk you are willing to take with your people and your career. It's a balancing act. If you chose criminal justice for security, how much are you willing to risk for that long-term security. If you have a spouse and family to support, are you willing to put their livelihood in harm's way?

Throughout this book, we tell you to get all of the education, training and experience that you can. How much of those elements you acquire can greatly influence your personal level of risk management? When you know and understand your job, and the system in which you work, it is much easier to assess the risks involved in any situation. You will know the law, you will know the case law on the topic, and you will follow your agency's policies and procedures. That generally puts you in a safe zone in making decisions. That's a good place to start from.

Then there are the other realities that you must also balance in your risk management assessments. Do you have a strong boss who will support your operational and ethical decisions? Will your decisions be politically correct in your agency or your municipality, *and* on the 6 o'clock news? What will be the effect of your decision on your relationships with your people, your peers, your bosses and the public? What effect might it have on your family in the short- and long-term?

Factoring in all these elements turns your simple oath of office to "uphold the law" into a complex ethical, socio-economic and political decision with far-reaching consequences. Now you know why criminal justice supervisors get paid so well!

So where do you stand on some of these issues, and how much risk are you willing to take? It's not an easy question and it requires some thought long before you face that angry mob or the smart politician. That's why we are bringing it to your attention now.

We can offer you a little more guidance to help you assess your level of risk management:

1. We have found that the more knowledge you have about your job, the better decisions you will make.

2. If you perform according to your agency's policies and procedures, you will generally be secure in your decision and the authority you used to make them.

3. Never commit your people to a task unless you have a 'reasonable expectation of winning'. That goes for physical **and** administrative confrontations.

4. Know the capabilities of all of the people and resources available to you.

5. Make time your ally to gather all the resources you need to be successful, both in the field, administratively and politically.

6. Document your actions at each stage of your endeavor.

7. Tell the truth in your reports, internal affairs investigations, court proceedings, etc.

8. Be sure that you made the best decision you could, based on your education, training and experience at the time and place, and under the circumstances that you found at that time. If anyone tries to second-guess you, gently remind them that you were there and they weren't. Trust us, they will seldom call you wrong.

In summary, the amount of risk you are willing to take in your career is entirely up to you and your circumstances in life. In general, high-risks result in high-stakes, and either high success or high failure. Low risks result in low stakes, and low success or failure consequences. It all depends on your comfort level.

Choose your own risk management level for your own career. After all, you are the one in charge of your career!

REVIEW QUESTIONS:

1. How could enforcing the laws and doing the "right thing" potentially hurt your criminal justice career?

2. Define "risk management." How does this term impact your decision-making as a career criminal justice professional?

3. List and explain at least five ways of assessing your level of risk management.

CHAPTER 25

Setting the Example

None of us can see ourselves as others see us. So how do your subordinates, peers and supervisors see you? Are they impressed by your appearance, demeanor, attitude and knowledge? Or, are you an example of everything that is wrong with the promotional system in your agency?

Well, let us first assure you that you cannot directly control the thoughts of members of any of these groups. Nor, should you necessarily try. However, you CAN take actions that are likely to influence other's opinions of you as an individual, as a criminal justice professional and as a valid member of your agency and community. Most of our suggestions are simple. Use them to be the best that you can be, not to necessarily influence others, but that will naturally follow.

Appearance

Dress appropriately for your position in your agency. Police and corrections officers have it relatively easy. They get to wear uniforms. Their job is to keep those uniforms properly cleaned, pressed and worn according to regulations.

Probation, parole, investigators and other criminal justice employees have it a little tougher. They are generally required to wear "appropriate business attire." Well, that can mean a wide variety of attire in today's business world. If specific guidelines are not provided, then we suggest leaning towards the more professional side of attire, consistent with what others in your agency wear. Not too trendy, but more traditional types of business attire usually work best. The criminal justice community tends to be more conservative and simple in their style of business attire. Yes, you can dress with your own individual style, but remember where you are working and with whom you are working. Dress so you can effectively fit in with your clients, your peers and your bosses.

Since the professional criminal justice community tends to be on the more conservative side, you may want to limit the amount of make-up, visible piercings, and tattoos that you have. Personal expression is great on your own personal time, but be sure to conform to your agency's rules, regulations and traditions if you want to be upwardly mobile.

Attitude

It has been said that attitude is everything in the workplace. We agree! You can view a glass as half-empty or half-full. You can accept your employer's rules as a condition of employment or you can constantly complain and try to circumvent them. You can view the criminal justice system as the best that we have at this time and place, and work within it, or you can constantly complain about it and make wrong choices on how you perform your job. You can be thankful that you have a secure job with a good benefit package and livable retirement or you can rail against your working conditions and become your agency's 'whiner'. It is all up to you.

Whichever attitude you choose will be recognized by your subordinates, your peers and your superiors. Now ask yourself this question: "If I want to get promoted, which attitude should I have—a positive one or a negative one?"

Physical fitness

By nature, many members of the criminal justice community will come into conflict with the criminal element of our society. Some of these confrontations will become physical, whether on the street, in a courtroom or in a correctional facility. So the question we ask you is: "Are you fit for duty?"

The public is often appalled at the grossly overweight and out-of-shape criminal justice employee. Hundreds of times we have been asked: "How can they chase somebody?" Well . . . we don't know.

But, once again, you as a criminal justice professional are being viewed and judged by your subordinates, your peers, your superiors and the public. If you were a commander looking for a fine example of what a criminal justice professional should be, would you choose one who was "fit for duty" or one who was not?

Knowledge

Respect is earned! Trust is earned! Subordinates respect and trust supervisors who have shown that they make the right decisions at the right times. These supervisors must know what to do, how to do it and when to do it. And, all of your subordinates, peers and superiors will have enough of their own knowledge and experience to make proper decisions in a timely manner. That makes for a smooth running shift and people who mutually respect each other. It's fun working in this kind of environment.

So, this segment on 'Setting the Example' is pretty simple. Look the part of a criminal justice professional and act like a criminal justice professional. In the process, you will be setting an example for your people, the public and other upwardly mobile officers in your agency. Those younger employees will tend to emulate your style of professionalism and that will make your job easier as their supervisor.

Onward and upward for all!

REVIEW QUESTIONS:

1. How do your subordinates, peers and superiors see you? (Be honest!)

2. What are some of the issues related to an employee's appearance?

3. What are some of the issues related to an employee's attitude? What are some of the issues related to an employee's physical fitness?

4. What are some of the issues related to an employee's job knowledge?

CHAPTER 26

Ethics

Law Enforcement Code of Ethics

Just in case you need some reminding, (or in case you didn't know), let us share with you what the International Association of Chiefs of Police has published regarding ethics:

"As a law enforcement officer, my fundamental duty is to serve mankind; to safeguard lives and property; to protect the innocent against deception; the weak against oppression or intimidation; and the peaceful against violence or disorder; and to respect the Constitutional rights of all men to liberty, equality, and justice.

I will keep my private life unsullied as an example to all; maintain courageous calm in the face of danger, scorn, or ridicule; develop self-restraint; and be constantly mindful of the welfare of others. Honest in my thought and deed in both personal and official life, I will be exemplary in obeying the laws of the land and the regulations of my department. Whatever I see, or hear, of a confidential nature or that is confided to me in my official capacity will be kept ever secret unless revelation is necessary in the performance of my duties.

I will never act officiously or permit personal feelings, prejudices, animosities, or friendships to influence my decisions. With no compromise for crime and with relentless prosecution of criminals, I will enforce the law courteously and appropriately without fear or favor, malice or ill-will, never employing unnecessary force or violence, and never accepting gratuities.

I recognize the badge of my office as a symbol of public faith, and I accept it as a public trust to be held so long as I am true to the ethics of police service. I will constantly strive to achieve these objectives and ideals, dedicating myself before God to my chosen profession—law enforcement."

Defining the problem

We don't have the time or space to delve into the philosophical nuances of utilitarianism, or deontological and teleological ethics, or Kant's view on morality. Instead, we will try to boil this large and complicated issue down to its most simplistic terms. Perhaps a basic definition is a good place to start: **Ethics** is derived from the Ancient Greek word *"ethikos,"* meaning "arising from habit," and deals with the analysis and application of such terms as "right," "wrong," "good," "evil" and "responsibility."

As it is with so many of the terms that we use in criminal justice, knowing the definition of a word is the easy part. It is the application and understanding of a word that is often a lot harder. For example, we all know what 'good and evil' are, and we know what 'right and wrong' is. But, apply these words to a basic scenario that is common on some oral board interviews that potential police officers face: "You are a police officer on patrol late at night and see a car roll through a stop sign and then weave back and forth as you begin to follow it. You stop the car, and determine that the operator is obviously intoxicated. You also determine that the operator is your father, and that he only lives two blocks from where you stopped him. What do you do?"

Of course we know what the law says, and we know what our sworn duty is, yet how many of us would arrest our father? Are you an unethical person for **not** arresting your father? Are you a 'good' police officer if you **do** arrest your father? Are you a 'good' police officer if you **don't** arrest your father? (And, the rebuttal that we often use in discussing these scenarios is: would you hire someone who **would** arrest their father?)

Remember the other part of this basic definition: . . . "arising from habit." We will talk about that later.

Perception versus reality

Some people claim that criminal justice is the "noblest" of professions. Others claim that the ". . . work by its very nature involves the slippery slope, the potential for gradual deterioration of socio-moral inhibitions and perceived sense of permissibility for deviant conduct."

Wow! Makes you wonder who is right. Of course, every time a criminal justice professional crosses the ethical/moral/legal line, and it makes big headlines in the media (and it *always* does . . .), it also makes the public wonder who is right. Are there thousands of criminal justice professionals out there who take advantage of the system every chance they get for their personal gain? Or, are there a much smaller number of individuals who cross the line, as they do in any occupation?

Does this battle between perception and reality affect you? Yes . . . every day! Do an Internet search of "criminal justice ethics" and you will get more than 11 million hits! We located a source that lists more than 850 codes of ethics from professional societies, corporations, government agencies, and academic institutions . . . Another example of the "perception versus reality" issue is reflected in a survey done by *Sourcebook of Criminal Justice Statistics*. When asked: "What is the most important problem facing this country today?," the choice picked most often by people was "morals and ethics," followed closely by "crime and violence." Whether real or perceived, these examples should show you how critical this topic is in both your personal and professional success.

Three ways of getting into ethical problems

There have been many research studies that have examined the issues related to criminal justice ethics. One way of looking at this will get you familiar with three terms that are important to discussing ethics.

1. *Malfeasance*—These acts would involve someone intentionally committing a prohibited act or doing something that he has no right. This could include a serious breach such as committing a crime on-duty or perjury, to lesser offenses that could involve violating your agency's policies, such as using your agency's resources for personal use.

   We often wonder whether it is audacity, foolishness or

some twisted version of logic that would make a criminal justice professional commit these types of egregious acts. Perhaps they think, like a lot of 'real' criminals that they won't get caught. However, if you look at these choices from an ethical standpoint, perhaps these individuals believe that a 'wrong' act can actually be the best ('right') choice. The fancy word for this is *'teleological ethics.'* An act may look bad, but if it results in 'good' consequences, then the act becomes 'good'. (Of course, then we have trouble defining the word 'good'.)

This makes sense if you apply it to a criminal investigation. A known child sexual predator is arrested again, after allegedly committing some very serious acts to a young child. In previous cases, the accused has been found not guilty, or plea bargained to a lesser charge or received a very light prison sentence. The detective investigating the case (the same detective who investigated the previous cases . . .) wants to be sure that this guy does not attack another child again. He plants evidence, or perjures himself, or violates the Constitutional rights of the accused, in order to guarantee a solid conviction. The conviction is gained and the person is sentenced to 25 years to life. Was a "greater good" for society done in this case, even though the means to getting this conviction was done illegally?

2. *Misfeasance*—This means that an employee is supposed to perform a duty or act, but does so in a manner that is improper, sloppy, or negligent.

Do any of your employees do sloppy work intentionally? Do they regularly break the minor rules of your agency, such as not writing a report when they are supposed to? Are they a little aggressive in handling incidents, especially if the incidents involve poor people, young people or any other group or individual that might indicate a bias by that employee? Do they stretch the limits of the law when conducting a search of a vehicle or of a person? If you question an employee on any of these acts, does he rationalize his behavior or come up with excuses? If you were to take a course on ethics, you would find this conduct maybe fits under the concept of "moral relativism."

3. *Nonfeasance*—This occurs when an employee fails to perform an act that he/she is obligated to do, either by law or directive due to omission or failure to recognize the obligation.

   In some cases, these incidents occur through a lack of understanding by the employee. Perhaps the employee failed to file a report when required by agency policy, or perhaps a search of a suspect was done improperly, or perhaps an employee violated a policy. Even though these breaches were done intentionally, they may not have been done deliberately. Does the employee know when to file a report, or how to conduct a search legally, or what the policy is that he violated? Is it lack of training, or lack of supervision, or a deliberate attempt by the employee to circumvent policies and training and intentionally commit a deviant act?

   There are many other ways of looking at the problems that poor choices contribute to ethical problems, but you have already figured out that any of these three categories of offenses can lead to serious problems for employees and supervisors.

What can go wrong?

It would be foolish to try and list all of the ways that criminal justice employees can get into ethical problems. The opportunities to commit deviant, unethical, corrupt or illegal acts confront many criminal justice professionals regularly. In spite of missing a few, allow us to list some of the major areas where poor decision-making by an employee can lead to serious consequences for them and for you.

- Any violation of the state laws should not be tolerated. (Taking a drug dealers money because he 'deserved it' is still stealing!)

- Violating agency policies. (Know what the rules are and follow them. Seems simple enough!)

- Accepting gratuities. (Let's not start the argument about whether accepting a free cup of coffee is 'corruption' or not. Instead, just don't put yourself in that position.)

- Shake-downs (any attempt to extort money from anyone is still a crime!)

- Failing to tell the truth. (Not just in court, either. One case we know of involved a long-time criminal justice employee who was fired for lying about where he was at a certain time when he was working. He was late for an important meeting and claimed that he got delayed because he made a motor vehicle stop. He lied, and was fired!)

- Using agency property or resources for personal use. (A long-time criminal justice employee was dismissed for taking a can of oil from the agency garage and putting it in his personal vehicle.)

- Sex-related incidents. (We are not talking about having an affair on duty [that's wrong, too!], but the more minor things like: a male police officer stopping all of the young, pretty female drivers to talk to them, or the voyeur who likes to sneak up on couples in "Lover's Lanes," or spending too much time in following up on crimes, especially when the victims are young and female, etc., etc.)

- Misuse of drugs or alcohol, on or off-duty—This is pretty self-explanatory

- ANY act that would bring dishonor, disrespect or shame to you, your family, friends, peers or the community if you got caught doing it! (I think that covers almost everything else you can think of!)

Conclusion

Once again, we do not bring you problems without bringing you solutions. The fact is that you, and your employees will regularly confront opportunities to make choices that may be unethical. You will have the opportunity to weigh the 'good' and the 'bad' for each decision that you make. Some of them will be easy to make . . . some will be difficult.

The best way to conclude this brief look at ethics is to offer you some excerpts from a speech that General Charles Krulak, former Commandant of the Marine Corps said in a speech in 1998. We ask that you think about each of these ideas and see how they fit into your actions and your own definition of ethics.

"Who are you? What do you stand for? What is the essence of your character? Where is your moral compass pointing?"

"The true test of character comes when the stakes are high, when the chips are down, when your gut starts to turn, when the sweat starts to form on your brow, when you know the decision you are about to make may not be popular . . . but it must be made."

"Those who have the courage to face up to ethical challenges in their daily lives will find that same courage can be drawn upon in times of great stress, in times of great controversy, in times of the never-ending battle between good and evil."

"All around our society, you see immoral behavior—lying, cheating, stealing, drug and alcohol abuse, prejudice and the lack of respect for human dignity and the law. Each of you will be confronted with situations where you will have to deal straight-up with issues such as these. The question is: what will you do when you are confronted with these issues? You will know what to do. The challenge is—will you DO what you know is right? It takes moral courage to hold your ideals above yourself. It is the DEFINING aspect. When the test of your character and moral courage comes—regardless of the noise and confusion around you—there will be a moment of inner silence in which you must decide what to do. Your character will be defined by your decision . . . and it is yours and yours alone to make."

REVIEW QUESTIONS:

1. What two important elements make up the basic function of the word "ethics"?

2. Discuss the moral, ethical and legal consequences of not arresting your father for driving while intoxicated.

3. How does a person's perception of reality differ from the reality of ethics?

4. Define the terms: malfeasance, misfeasance and non-feasance.

5. List at least five major areas where poor decision-making can lead to serious consequences.

CHAPTER 27

Career Development

Where do you want to be in your career in five years . . . in ten years . . . in twenty years? What will you want to do when you retire from your current job?

Although all of these dates seem a long way off, it is what you do *now* that will determine your future. You can do nothing and leave your career to chance, or you can take charge of your career and thereby take control of much of your destiny. The phrase: "If it is to be, it is up to me," will never have greater meaning.

So, it is time to sit down and do some planning for your future, and for your family's future. Answer the question that we first asked you. Where do you want to be in five years . . . in ten years . . . in twenty years? To answer that properly, you must take into consideration your own desires, goals and obligations. Your children may need help with college tuition about the time you are thinking about retiring. There is a big difference in retirement pay between patrol officer and chief. You may choose a different career path than one of your co-workers, but each of you can still be successful as long as you follow a career development plan.

Sit down and start planning your future. You may change it later, as things come up in your personal and professional life, but at least you have a plan to work from. If you want to remain as a line-worker (police officer, probation officer, etc.), there is nothing wrong with that, as long as you plan on being the best that you can be in that position. But, putting two or three kids through college might be tough on that salary, and early retirement is usually not feasible on a patrol officer's salary. But, you decide.

Going up the career ladder of many progressive criminal justice agencies may require a significant investment for you in education, training and experience. That path may involve working longer hours, spending your off-duty time going to college instead of with your family, frequent transfers in larger agencies, and increased levels of stress. But then, the pay and benefits are generally much greater, your retirement compensation will be much higher, and your chances of leaving your present job for a higher-paying "retirement" job are much greater.

Let's see if we can help you make some of these tough decisions:

1. *Where do you want to go?*

One nice thing about the criminal justice profession is that you have so many career paths available to you. For example, in policing, you can go into specialty areas such as; investigations, K-9, bomb squad, school resource officer, accident investigation, etc. or you can choose to go through the supervisory ranks. So, what do you want to do? Obviously the more diverse your background, the more desirable you are as an employee.

But keep in mind, applying for any specialized position is often competitive and management may want to "reward" the better employee, the more motivated employee, the most active employee, the one who has "earned" the position. Does this sound like you? If not, you had better change your attitude, your work ethic and your reputation as an employee now!

2. *What education do you need?*

In supervisory ranks, although unwritten in most agencies, an associate's degree in criminal justice or a related field is the minimum required just to get hired at entry level. (And of course, many larger agencies or specific positions in the field require a Bachelor's degree.) From that, it only makes sense that first-line supervisors might be expected to have a Bachelor's Degree, mid-level managers would have a Master's Degree and ranks above that would have additional specialized courses. At any rank, formal degrees can give you greater credibility and allow you a greater understanding of your role in the criminal justice system in relation to everyone else in the field.

3. *What training do you need?*

Regardless of which career path you choose, you can never have too much training. Every training course will give you knowledge that you can draw on to solve problems that you may face in your career. Seek out training programs both within and outside of your agency. If you choose a specialty career path such as forensics, K-9 or investigations, be sure that you attend the best training programs that you can find. Again, your credibility may depend on your level of training in these specialty areas.

We remind you that many agencies have limited training budgets or administrators may be reluctant to send employees to any training that is not required. Successful career-minded employees may choose to go on their own time, spend their own money and develop their own careers with or without the support of the agencies. You should consider spending a couple of hundred dollars, or burning a few vacation days, to go to a desirable training seminar as investing in your future, and nothing is more important than that.

4. *What experience do you need to succeed?*

There is no substitute for experience in a given area. You can learn the basics, and maybe even a few tricks in the classroom or from a book, but the true test comes from experience in the field. Forensic chemists learn more than chemistry in the lab. Court officers learn the realities of the interactions with judges and lawyers only through experience. Bomb squad technicians learn not to move too quickly, or when to move really fast! Whatever career path you choose, determine what experience you need to maximize your success and show your true potential. Some supervisors like to supervise the most challenging units or the busiest units. That way, they can show that they can handle any unit and any task. Some investigators like to go where the action is to use their investigative skills to the fullest.

Of course, as you can figure out, there may be some risk involved in taking this plan of action. You may put yourself and your reputation on the line, especially when failure might impact your career. Do you have the confidence, the knowledge, the skills and the abilities to make it work? Some employees view these situations as risky, while others view them as opportunities. You know the old saying about opportunity knocking . . . ?

So you have the general idea that you need the right combination of education, training and experience to achieve the positions that you want for a successful career. Now what? Here are a few more tips to help you enjoy a long and successful career:

1. *Get a friend*

   Some people call them mentors, others call them "godfathers," others call them more generic names. In general, they are successful and upwardly mobile professionals, usually in the chain of command above you, who recognize your potential and want to help you succeed. Often, they will seek you out, but only *after* you have demonstrated your enthusiasm, interest and an above-average ability to get the job done. (*Warning*: these mentors do not have the time or interest to work with mediocre or average employees. No matter how much you want their help, you need to prove that you have what it takes to succeed.)

   Just as we told you that it is your job as a supervisor to develop future leaders in your unit, it is their responsibility to help you succeed for the good of the organization. Listen to them, take their advice and give back to others in kind when you succeed.

2. *Join professional associations*

   There are professional associations for virtually every specialty career path in criminal justice. There are associations for drug investigators, gang units, juvenile drug counselors, trainers, dispatchers, police chiefs, etc., etc. There are more than we can list here.

   Find out what is out there in your field. Most have newsletters or magazines, training seminars, websites that can keep you up-to-date on new equipment, tactics, laws and procedures. Spend a few dollars a year to join these associations. Most of your competition in your agency will not, and that can give you an advantage in planning your career.

3. *Teach*

"He who teaches—learns!" Some of you are taking all of the steps necessary to be the best in your chosen career path, so it is only natural that you should teach your profession to others. Criminal justice training academies and colleges are often looking for people with your kind of professional expertise and experience to teach courses or at least be a guest speaker. It is a great way to share your knowledge and get recognized as an expert by people both within and outside of your agency. And, of course, it looks good on your resume.

4. *Write*

Remember those professional associations that we just mentioned? Well, almost every one of them has a newsletter or journal that they send to all their members. The editors of these publications are always looking for professionals to write articles on new tactics, training or equipment. If you can write, look into writing an article and don't hesitate to send it in for review. It can get you and your department national recognition and looks great on your resume. (**Caution:** Check with your organization to be sure that you are allowed to write such articles, You may need permission in advance.)

Okay, so you are now done preparing your career plan. Well . . . almost. We want to give you a few more tips and options to factor into your career plan.

1. *Avoid over-specialization*

Becoming the best K-9 officer in the region is great. And, if that is all you ever want to do, and can afford that career path, then do so. But, it is almost impossible to transition from K-9 officer to police chief. You get the idea. So spend some time as a K-9 officer, school resource officer, trainer, accident investigator. Work hard at each opportunity and become very good at each opportunity you are given. But, understand that there are few, if any, higher paying ranks for those positions and you may not have advancement opportunities if you stay in any specialized area too long.

It almost sounds like a "no-win" situation—here we are encouraging you to become the best at what you do, and liking your job is important for motivation and good mental health, yet if you become too good at a job, your agency may think you are "too valuable" to promote or transfer. You may also become labeled as only being good in one specific area. None of these is good for career development.

2. *Assess your risk level*

Certainly a career in criminal justice may involve some physical risks. But, also be aware of other types of career risks that may arise from mistakes, supervisor responsibilities and other decisions that you make along the way. You also need to include stress as a risk factor. Then, consider your own comfort level of risk, perhaps your family's risk level and the consequences that you and they may face if it all goes wrong one day. Factor that into any career decisions that you make.

3. *Do you have the will to lead?*

Some people like to lead, and some are much more comfortable following the leader. The criminal justice profession needs both types of people. If you enjoy being out in front, challenging yourself to accomplish the difficult tasks and don't mind being the target of "slings and arrows" from various sources, then decide to become a leader. The rewards are great, and you help your subordinates reach their goals and go up through the ranks themselves. The pay is better, there are greater benefits, your retirement package improves and you improve your chances of a successful second career. But, there are risks involved in being the one responsible at crime scenes or making difficult supervisory or management decisions or a myriad of other things that can occur in your career as you go up the ladder. You decide if you have the "will to lead." If not, it is okay. But keep in mind that you cannot succeed as a criminal justice supervisor without that "will to lead."

Okay. So now you have many of the factors necessary to plan out your career. Think about it, discuss it with your family, check with friends and mentors and retired criminal justice professionals who have been successful. You may want to consult a financial planner, accountant or life insurance agent as you work on your career plan. But, the most important thing is that you have a plan. Without a plan, any mission is doomed to fail. And, your career is much too important to risk failure for lack of a well-thought-out plan for your future and the future of your family.

REVIEW QUESTIONS:

1. What are two reasons why formal education can be important in a criminal justice career?

2. Why do you need a career plan?

3. Of what value are professional associations to your career?

4. Why should you avoid over-specialization in your career plan?

5. What is meant by the "will to lead"?

CHAPTER 28

Your "Running Resume"

"What, if any, qualifications do you have to be in your current position?" a sharp attorney asks you as you take the witness stand in a Superior Court case in which you are accused of failing to actively supervise the members of your unit at a critical incident. You might stammer and stutter and finally blurt out that you attended the basic training school, and then mention that you went to a couple of in-service training classes, but you can't remember exactly when. Or . . . you can confidently pull out your "running resume" that lists all of your education, training and experience, as well as a list of your commendations, promotions and other past accomplishments. The lawyer may even ask that your "running resume" be admitted into evidence, so that the jury can review it later. Which of these scenarios do you think is most impressive to the judge, lawyers and jury?

The 'running resume' requires a little work on your part initially, but then just needs to be reviewed every six months or so, and changes made whenever a new item should be added. In order to prepare your 'running resume', you will first need to gather all the documentation you can find in regards to the following topics pertaining to your career:

1. *Education*—Colleges attended and degrees achieved. If you do not have a college degree, just list the college courses you have taken. You might even use the phrase "enrolled in a criminal justice degree program." Of course, it would be impressive to include a high grade point average, too.

2. *Training*—Basic, in-service and specialized training courses should be listed here. It doesn't matter whether

your agency sponsored them or not, as long as they are related to the criminal justice field. Check with your training officer or personnel officer for an accurate record. Be sure to keep any documentation or certificates that you receive from any training that you attend.

3. *Positions held*—List all of the various positions that you have held in your career. Try to show progressively more supervisory or administrative experience. Titles such as Assistant Shift Commander, Acting Program Coordinator, Director of a Project, and any others, can be as valid as a title of Sergeant or Supervisor to show your basic and supervisory experience.

4. *Commendations*—List all that you can, from the letter of appreciation for changing a motorist's tire, or for working especially hard for one of your clients, to any formal commendations that you have received (Employee of the Year, Medal of Valor, etc.) Juries **love** commendations!

5. *Affiliations*—List the professional criminal justice associations that you are a member of. These can include any local, state or national professional criminal justice organization. If you do not belong to any . . . join some! Leave off the fraternal, religious or union affiliations. Also, if you subscribe to any professional criminal justice journals, this is the place to list them. If you don't subscribe to any, then you had better start!

6. *Publications*—Whether you wrote an article for your local newspaper or a book on forensics, list it here. Publications give you credibility.

Once you have accumulated all of the documentation in each area, put it together in a standard resume format of your choosing. The format, categories and appearance should be professional looking. Put it into a computer file so that you can quickly and easily make changes as you continue to expand your education, training and experience.

The most important thing is that you prepare and maintain your 'running resume' for presentation to juries, promotional boards or any unexpected time when you need it. Trust us, attorneys will be shocked at your preparation, and promotional boards will be pleasantly surprised and duly influenced. Both groups will admire your professionalism.

Your 'running resume' should be reviewed and amended annually, at a minimum, or whenever a significant event occurs in your career such as a promotion, completion of a training course, new position, etc. If an oral board assessment requires a resume, you will be ready to present one at a moment's notice. Your competition may not have prepared as well as you, and you will win the day.

To be successful and promotable in the field of criminal justice requires a great deal of preparation and development. You can prepare yourself through education, training and experience. However, to be truly successful, you must reach out to other areas to prove yourself and be recognized as a truly effective and competent leader in the criminal justice community.

REVIEW QUESTIONS:

1. Explain how a running resume can enhance your credibility as a criminal justice professional.

2. List the six main components of a running resume.

3. List at least three opportunities where having a running resume would be important to your career.

CHAPTER 29

Planning a Successful "Retirement" Career

This is a career development book. And, it is a fact that your career in your current criminal justice agency will not last forever. The demands and stresses of many criminal justice jobs have been recognized and retirement is common after only 20 or 25 years of service in some jobs. In most cases, retirement is voluntary. In some cases, your retirement may be premature and involuntary. Physical injuries, health problems, off-duty conduct, and politics can all be responsible for early retirements, or a premature end to a criminal justice career. And, the events involved in a forced retirement can happen with amazing speed.

With all that in mind, the goal of being prepared for your inevitable retirement is not necessarily in opposition to your success in your current position. In fact, the goals of the two positions can easily be the same. Properly preparing yourself for your current and future positions within your own agency may actually be preparing you for your working life after you retire, whether to another criminal justice position or into the private sector.

Planning ahead

We hope it never happens to you, but suppose that you are headed to work tomorrow and are involved in a serious auto accident that leaves you too disabled to continue in your criminal justice career. What will you do next? How will you support your family? What will your future look like?

Those are sobering thoughts, but they are thoughts that you and your loved ones should plan for. There are many other types of accidents and events that can quickly end a criminal justice career. The most forward-looking members of the criminal justice community recognize that they will be entering into a second career, involuntarily, or through the retirement system, at an undetermined point in the future. In most cases that will mean taking another job, maybe in criminal justice and maybe not, and working under a different set of rules than the paramilitary environment of most criminal justice agencies.

Work hard, now!

Have you heard the saying: "You get out of life what you put into it"? Well, you will get out of your career what you put into it. Take a look at the people that you work with. Does it seem like certain people get all "the breaks"—they get the promotions, they get the special assignments, they get sent to training classes . . . they end up with a successful career, and they roll over into a very successful second career after they retire. Well, they don't end up with a successful career based on their good looks, wit and charm—no . . . they get there after years of hard work.

Why should your boss send you to a training class, or try to get you promoted, or give you a desirable appointment to a special detail if you are only an "average" employee? There are LOTS of "average" employees in criminal justice . . . just take a look around your agency! There is nothing wrong with spending an entire career being "average," but if you are an "average" employee, you should only expect to have an "average" career. Successful people are seldom average—no matter what job they have. Successful people are always trying to get better at what they do, they are always doing a little bit more than what is expected, they are always pushing themselves a little harder. They don't want an "average" career. You shouldn't, either!

Transferring your skills

You should recognize that many of the attributes that have made you successful in your current work are readily transferable to other jobs. These include your ability to get the job done, your discipline and your enthusiasm. Both the public and private sectors need people with these attributes. Private companies and businesses are always looking for honest, dedicated, disciplined, professional employees at all levels. Take inventory of your skills and attributes and you will feel very confident about your ability to succeed in another career.

Throughout this book, we have encouraged you to expand your knowledge, skills and abilities. Hopefully, you will have the opportunity to hold several different job titles during your career that will allow you to develop different job skills. Try to plan your career so that some of these job skills would be transferable to private sector jobs. Criminal justice employees who spend too many years specializing in one or two job tasks (especially if they have limited transferability), may find limited employment opportunities in their second career. For example, a long-time commander of a SWAT team, or someone who worked many years in undercover narcotics investigations, would have many fascinating stories to tell about their various experiences, but there would not be many jobs in the private sector that would need those skills. However, criminal justice professionals who develop a broad-based resume that would include a variety of skills and knowledge would be more adaptable to the private sector.

One of the most important skill areas that you should work on during your current career are "people skills." Many criminal justice employees work with people every day—but, of course, there is a big difference in how a police officer would handle a convicted drug-dealer in a dark alley, or how a correction officer would handle an uncooperative inmate, compared to how professsional people handle clients in the private sector. Add "effective people skills" to some of the skills that you are currently developing—good decision-making, honesty, integrity, high motivation, ethics, etc.—and this could open many doors for you in your second career.

Prepare yourself for your second career

Throughout this book, we have encouraged you to take charge of your career, plan for your promotions and combine education, training and experience in your criminal justice career. We also want you to do that for your second career.

(**Note:** We HATE the word "retirement." We avoid using it. We think it is a 'passive' word. We have seen too many people dread retiring because they don't have anything else to do. They did not plan for a second career. Their whole world revolves around "the job." They try to desperately hang on to their current job because without it—they don't have anything to give meaning to their life. Often these people become sad and lonely people when they "retire." So—DON'T RETIRE!!! But *do* plan on working your way into a great second career that could be more rewarding, more challenging, and more lucrative than your first career!)

Even if you've been to every training class that your agency offers, even if you have achieved rank and responsibility in your career, even if you have a file folder full of commendations . . . it may not be enough to "retire" to a successful second career. The world is changing out there—beyond the little criminal justice world that you have lived in for the past twenty or thirty years. Here are a couple of things you can do to help you transition into a successful second career:

1. Find a hobby or a job outside of criminal justice that you enjoy doing. Get really good at it! You can hone your skills in the evenings at home instead of watching re-runs of sit-coms on television.

    One guy we know loved to play golf, but wasn't really good at it. But, he did like the idea of being 'around' golf when he retired, so he began working part-time at a golf course in the pro shop while he was still 'on the job.' He learned about inventory, sales, accounting, how to run golf tournaments, etc., and after he retired, he began a second career as a golf course manager. Last we knew, he was working in an exclusive golf resort area of the country. Another guy we knew turned a woodworking hobby into a very lucrative second career making special order wooden furniture.

2. Become the best you can at what you do now, and then turn that into a second career. It is no surprise to any of you that there is a big market in the private sector for people who have skills in such areas as accident investigation, polygraph, arson investigation, etc., etc.

You could get hired by an insurance company, a private investigation company, a law firm, become a private consultant, become an expert witness, write a book, become a training consultant—you get the idea! But . . . all of this is predicated on a couple of things. First, you have to get the training initially. Second, you have to become VERY good at what it is you are trained at (mediocrity is not accepted in the private sector). And third, you have to prepare yourself for your second career long before you actually retire from your first career.

But, if you are going to have a successful career as a private consultant or working in private business, you may have to acquire some additional skill. See the next item for more thoughts on this.

3. Work on new skills NOW that will help you transition into a lucrative second career. For example, you may know how to run your agency's report incident software program better than anybody in your agency, but . . . what good will that do in your second career?

    Computer skills are critical in any job, but your second-career employer would much rather have you proficient at Excel or Peachtree, rather than your agency's case management software program. You may have to go back to college and take some courses OTHER THAN criminal justice courses to prepare for your second career. Take some computer courses, take some teaching courses, take some writing courses, take some business courses, take any course that will give you new skills to add to your 'running resume'.

4. Meet new people. We hope you have mastered the skill of networking during your criminal justice career. The value of this cannot be measured, and will go far in making your career in criminal justice successful. However, you need to *really* start networking outside of your criminal justice circle when you start planning for your second career.

    Reach out to people in your community that you may not have had the opportunity to deal with as you have spent the past twenty or thirty years in your little niche called "criminal justice." Some of this outreach can be done at the same time that you are working on your current career. For example, if you wanted to develop your public speaking skills, we suggested earlier in this book that you might consider joining "Toastmasters International." Well, while you are at their meetings and developing skills to help your current job, you will meet professional people in your community from all walks of life and all different jobs doing the same thing. A chance conversation with one of them could lead you to a career that you never expected.

We have found that joining certain organizations or going to places where professional people hang-out is a good place to meet professional people that you would normally never associate with. These could include: joining a civic group, start attending events at your nearby college, join a health club, become a member of any type of outdoor club (hiking club, running club, biking club, etc.), join professional associations related to your hobby, do charity work in your community, join your local community theater, etc. Go out of your way to meet professional people in your community!

It's all about making your own opportunities, and taking charge of your career—now, and for the rest of your life!

REVIEW QUESTIONS:

1. List some specific skills that you should develop now that will be transferable into a second career.

2. List at least three ways you can help yourself transition into a successful second career.

3. List some specific steps that you need to take to prepare yourself for a second career.

CHAPTER 30

Conclusion

Don't think that your work is done just because you've finished reading this book!

You have a job to do!

You have a career to take charge of!

Even the best criminal justice agency in the world (. . . you probably don't work there, do you?) will not take care of your career the way your career should be taken care of. No one that you will ever work for will care more about your career than you should. Therefore, it makes sense that you need to carefully plan your career . . . for your sake . . . for the sake of your future . . . for the sake of your family.

We have seen some criminal justice employees have amazingly successful careers. And, we have also seen some criminal justice careers 'crash and burn'. Is there that much of a difference between those that 'did' and those that 'didn't'? We think the answer to that question is—YES!

Successful people, and that includes successful criminal justice professionals, all tend to have some basic things in common:

1. They have a high level of motivation
2. They have a good work ethic
3. They have an inner drive to excel, personally and professionally.
4. They have the ability to adapt to changing conditions
5. They don't make excuses—they overcome obstacles

If you feel comfortable saying: "I've got that," after every item on this short list, then there should be no reason why you cannot have a successful career in criminal justice, and beyond.

Throughout this book, we have challenged you to take charge of your career. It's simple. You have a choice—take control or lose control.

We sincerely convey our best wishes that you may have a long and successful career in the criminal justice field.

Mike and Roger

Index